T0278464

THE
LEADERSHIP CHALLENGE WORKBOOK

THE
LEADERSHIP
CHALLENGE
WORKBOOK

DESIGNED TO ACCOMPANY THE AWARD-WINNING BOOK, *THE LEADERSHIP CHALLENGE*

JAMES M. | BARRY Z.

KOUZES | POSNER

THE
LEADERSHIP
CHALLENGE
WORKBOOK

FOURTH EDITION

HOW TO MAKE

EXTRAORDINARY THINGS HAPPEN

IN ORGANIZATIONS

Copyright © 2023 by James M. Kouzes and Barry Z. Posner. All rights reserved.

Published by John Wiley & Sons, Inc., Hoboken, New Jersey.
Published simultaneously in Canada.

No part of this publication may be reproduced, stored in a retrieval system, or transmitted in any form or by any means, electronic, mechanical, photocopying, recording, scanning, or otherwise, except as permitted under Section 107 or 108 of the 1976 United States Copyright Act, without either the prior written permission of the Publisher, or authorization through payment of the appropriate per-copy fee to the Copyright Clearance Center, Inc., 222 Rosewood Drive, Danvers, MA 01923, (978) 750-8400, fax (978) 750-4470, or on the web at www.copyright.com. Requests to the Publisher for permission should be addressed to the Permissions Department, John Wiley & Sons, Inc., 111 River Street, Hoboken, NJ 07030, (201) 748-6011, fax (201) 748-6008, or online at http://www.wiley.com/go/permission.

Trademarks: Wiley and the Wiley logo are trademarks or registered trademarks of John Wiley & Sons, Inc. and/or its affiliates in the United States and other countries and may not be used without written permission. All other trademarks are the property of their respective owners. John Wiley & Sons, Inc. is not associated with any product or vendor mentioned in this book.

Limit of Liability/Disclaimer of Warranty: While the publisher and author have used their best efforts in preparing this book, they make no representations or warranties with respect to the accuracy or completeness of the contents of this book and specifically disclaim any implied warranties of merchantability or fitness for a particular purpose. No warranty may be created or extended by sales representatives or written sales materials. The advice and strategies contained herein may not be suitable for your situation. You should consult with a professional where appropriate. Further, readers should be aware that websites listed in this work may have changed or disappeared between when this work was written and when it is read. Neither the publisher nor authors shall be liable for any loss of profit or any other commercial damages, including but not limited to special, incidental, consequential, or other damages.

For general information on our other products and services or for technical support, please contact our Customer Care Department within the United States at (800) 762-2974, outside the United States at (317) 572-3993 or fax (317) 572-4002.

Wiley also publishes its books in a variety of electronic formats. Some content that appears in print may not be available in electronic formats. For more information about Wiley products, visit our web site at www.wiley.com.

Library of Congress Cataloging-in-Publication Data

Names: Kouzes, James M., 1945- author. | Posner, Barry Z., author. |
   Kouzes, James M., 1945- Leadership challenge.
Title: The leadership challenge workbook / James M. Kouzes, Barry Z.
   Posner.
Description: Fourth Edition. | Hoboken, New Jersey : Wiley, [2023] |
   Revised edition of the authors' The leadership challenge workbook,
   c2012.
Identifiers: LCCN 2022061226 (print) | LCCN 2022061227 (ebook) | ISBN
   9781394152223 (paperback) | ISBN 9781394152247 (adobe pdf) | ISBN
   9781394152230 (epub)
Subjects: LCSH: Leadership. | Executive ability. | Management.
Classification: LCC HD57.7 .K6815 2023 (print) | LCC HD57.7 (ebook) | DDC
   658.4092—dc23/eng/20221222
LC record available at https://lccn.loc.gov/2022061226
LC ebook record available at https://lccn.loc.gov/2022061227

Cover Design: Wiley
Cover Image: Lake Bachalpsee © aCZhou / Getty Images
Author Photos: Courtesy of the Authors

SKY10079035_070824

Contents

Contents

INTRODUCTION

WHEN WE INTERVIEWED DON BENNETT for our first book, he said something that we've never forgotten. Don is the first amputee to climb Mount Rainier. That's 14,410 feet on one leg and two crutches.

"How did you make it to the top?" we asked Don.

"One hop at a time," was his instant reply.

One hop at a time. One hop at a time. One hop at a time.

When you think about it, that's how most extraordinary things are accomplished. As much as you might desire it, you simply cannot leap to the top of a mountain. You can only get there by taking it one step—or, as in Don's case—one hop at a time.

Yet we sometimes find ourselves simply paralyzed by the mere scale of the challenge. We are challenged to do more with less, adapt quickly to changing circumstances, innovate on the fly, deal with extreme uncertainty, and somehow still find time for our families and friends. Sometimes it all feels too overwhelming. But so does looking up to the top of a mountain when you are at the bottom. That's why Don would tell himself, as he looked just one foot ahead, "Anybody can hop from here to there." And so he did—fourteen thousand four hundred ten times.

But Don had something else in mind when he looked up at the top of that mountain. Despite what you might have heard about why people climb mountains, it's not because they're there. When we asked Don why he wanted to be the first amputee to climb Mount Rainier, he told us it was because he wanted to demonstrate to other disabled people that they were capable of doing more than they might have thought they could do. Don had aspirations that went beyond individual glory and success. He was the one doing the climbing, but he was not climbing just for himself. He was climbing for an entire community. He had a vision of others doing great things.

There's another lesson we learned from Don that's directly applicable to leading others to make extraordinary things happen. We asked him, "What's the most important lesson you learned from this climb?" Without hesitation, he answered, "You can't do it alone."

We produced *The Leadership Challenge Workbook* so that you can apply to your projects the leadership lessons we learned from Don Bennett—and from the thousands of other leaders we have studied. This is a practical guide that is designed to help you use The Five Practices of Exemplary Leadership®—the model of leadership derived from, and validated by, more than forty years of research—as a tool for planning and preparing for your next climb to the summit.

The Leadership Challenge Workbook is a one-hop-at-a-time guide for leaders. It's a tool that asks you to reflect on each essential element of leading and to act in ways that incrementally create forward momentum. It asks you to think beyond your personal agenda and imagine how your leadership efforts engage others' desires. Because you can't do it alone, it also helps you engage others in the planning and the doing.

ARE YOU LEADING AT YOUR "PERSONAL BEST"?

When we began our research, we wanted to find out what practices characterize exemplary leadership, so we created a question that framed everything else. The question we asked everyone we studied was, "What did you do when you were at your 'personal best' as a leader?" We did not want to know what the most famous and the most senior leaders did. We wanted to know what leaders at *all* levels and in all contexts did. We asked people to tell us a story about the one project they led that they considered their Personal-Best Leadership Experience—an experience that set their individual standard of excellence. We collected thousands of stories of leaders performing at their peak, and we looked for actions that were consistent across all the stories.

After many years—and several thousand quantitative and qualitative analyses—we found that there are Five Practices that define exemplary leadership. When operating at their best, leaders:

- Model the Way
- Inspire a Shared Vision
- Challenge the Process
- Enable Others to Act
- Encourage the Heart

You might already be familiar with The Five Practices from our book *The Leadership Challenge,* which describes this research in detail. Or you might know The Five Practices because you have used our 360-degree assessment instrument, the *Leadership Practices Inventory* (LPI), to further your development as a leader. In case the practices are new to you, we provide a brief overview in Chapter 2 of this workbook.

Whether or not you are familiar with our other work, we ask you to keep this in mind: when you engage in The Five Practices more frequently than you do at present, you *will* be more effective. We know from our research that those who Model, Inspire, Challenge, Enable, and Encourage more frequently significantly increase their probability of making extraordinary things happen. Exemplary leadership, in other words, is not an accident of birth or circumstance. It's a result of conscious and conscientious practice.

PROJECTS PROVIDE THE CONTEXT

Projects are how we tend to organize work these days. Projects create the context for our goals, determine with whom we work, and set our schedules. We will be more specific in Chapter 3 about what kind of project to use as the framework for applying The Five Practices while you go through this workbook. But you might start thinking now about one that you are currently leading or about to lead that could benefit from the application of exemplary practices.

One important point to keep in mind is that every new project provides you with an opportunity. It's an opportunity to do things the same way you have always done them, or it's an opportunity for greatness—an opportunity to achieve a personal standard of excellence. It all depends on how you approach the challenge.

No world-class athlete ever set foot on the playing field saying to themselves, "I think I'll settle for performing at my average today." The same is true of world-class leaders. Every day is an opportunity to improve your performance, and the most challenging projects are the ones that create the most opportunity. Your next project is your chance to create extraordinary results for your organization and to develop your leadership capabilities. This workbook is designed to help you plan and prepare so that you can lead at your personal best.

WHO SHOULD USE THE LEADERSHIP CHALLENGE WORKBOOK?

This workbook is designed for anyone in a leadership role. Its purpose is to help you further your abilities to lead others in making extraordinary things happen. Whether you are in the private or public sector, an employee or a volunteer, a first-line supervisor or a senior executive, a student or a parent, you will find that this workbook applies to you. That's because leadership is not about being in a formal position. It's about action. You can grant someone the title of manager, but that does not make them a leader. Leadership is earned.

You get to be a leader in the eyes of others because of what you *do*. Leadership is about having the courage and spirit to move from whatever circumstances you are in to a place of making a difference in the world. This workbook is designed to help anyone who has the desire to lead and the will to make a difference. It's for anyone who is in a role that requires mobilizing others to want to struggle for shared aspirations.

LEADERSHIP IS EVERYONE'S BUSINESS

The next time you say to yourself, "Why don't they do something about that?" look in the mirror. Ask the person you see, "Why don't *you* do something about that?" By accepting the challenge to lead, you come to realize that the only limits are those you place on yourself.

While our research has taught us many things about the practice of leadership, our interaction with the thousands of individuals we have studied has taught us something vitally important: leadership is everyone's business. In today's rapidly changing, highly competitive, increasingly global world, we need more leaders, not fewer. We need more people to accept responsibility for bringing about significant changes in what we do and how we do it. We need more people to answer the call. The world is in great need of your talents.

We believe that you are capable of developing yourself as a leader far more than tradition or mythology has ever assumed possible. Simply imagine yourself standing at the base of Mount Rainier, and then start climbing—one hop at a time.

We wish you great joy and success on your next leadership adventure.

Jim Kouzes, Orinda, California
Barry Posner, Berkeley, California
2023

CHAPTER 1

How to Use This Workbook

THE BEST LEADERS ARE CONTINUALLY LEARNING. They see all experiences as learning opportunities. But there's one condition. Rich insights only come from reflection and analysis. Unexamined experiences yield no lessons. If you want to become a better leader, you need to study your own performance and become more conscious about the choices that you are making and how you are acting on your intentions.

The purpose of *The Leadership Challenge Workbook* is to help you become a better leader by applying The Five Practices of Exemplary Leadership® to a project of your choice. As with the learning of any new discipline, we will ask you to do some exercises that isolate specific skills. This may seem a bit artificial at first, but it's no different from any form of practice—you are not actually in the game, but you know you are improving your capacity to play the game.

HOW THE WORKBOOK IS ORGANIZED

In Chapter 2 we've provided a summary of The Five Practices model that resulted from our forty-plus years of research. If you've read *The Leadership Challenge* or have used the *Leadership Practices Inventory*, you may not need to review the model, but it's there if you need a reminder. If you are not already familiar with The Five Practices, read that chapter carefully—it provides the foundation for the work that you will be doing.

Chapter 3 offers some guidelines for choosing the right leadership project. To enable you to focus your work, it's essential that you select a real project to serve as the target of your reflections, applications, and actions.

In Chapters 4 through 8, you'll apply The Five Practices to that project. And in Chapter 9, which you'll complete after your project is finished (or well underway), you will find questions that will help you reflect on the project's highs and lows and on what you learned—lessons you can then apply to your next Personal Best Leadership Project.

As you progress through the activities, the workbook supports your success in three ways:

1. *Reflection.* We want you to think about how you approach leadership. The questions we pose are designed to challenge your thinking and help you become more conscious about how well you engage in each of The Five Practices. Contrary to myths about leadership that assume you either have it or you don't, we know from our research that the very best leaders spend time examining what they have done as well as what they are planning to do. Call it the "mental game of leadership." The exercises in this workbook ask you to be more reflective about what your experience can teach you about leadership.
2. *Application.* We want you to apply the leadership practices and commitments to your project. To do that, we provide exercises that help put The Five Practices of Exemplary Leadership® to work. In some cases you will do this application alone. In other cases, you will talk with your team members and engage them in an activity.
3. *Implications.* As a result of your reflections and applications, you will learn about yourself, your team, your organization, and your project. At the end of each chapter, we ask you to write down the implications of what you have learned about leadership.

GUIDELINES FOR COMPLETING THE WORKBOOK

It would be ideal if you could complete the entire workbook as a way of preparing yourself and everyone involved in the project—somewhat like a series of warm-up exercises before playing the game. On a practical level, that may not be possible. The way you use the workbook depends on the nature of your project and your situation. Here are some suggestions:

- If you're just starting your project, we recommend that you begin with Chapter 4, Model the Way, and work your way through Chapter 8, Encourage the Heart.

- If your project has been underway for some time, we recommend that you begin by reading through this workbook quickly, without doing the activities. Then go back and start with those worksheets that address your immediate concerns. For example, your team might have been working long hours without a break, and you believe that they need some recognition and celebration. In that case, start with Chapter 8, Encourage the Heart. You may feel that conflicts have arisen because there is insufficient consensus around shared values. If so, begin with Chapter 4, Model the Way. Or you may find that some questions are richer and more useful to you than others. We encourage you to proceed through this book in whatever way resonates for you. However, make sure you address all The Five Practices and complete all the activities as soon as you can. They are designed to improve the way you lead.

- You may find that you have already completed some of the activities that are in this workbook. For instance, you and your team may have spent a lot of time identifying and agreeing upon your shared values. If you have already done something equivalent to what's in this workbook, pause long enough to make sure you are comfortable with what you have done and do not need to revisit it. Then move on to the next activity.

- This is important, however: no matter how you use the workbook, we urge you not to skip over any of the leadership practices.

As you do the activities, you may sometimes find yourself saying, "I don't know." For example, when we ask, "Who's on your project team?" you may initially answer, "I don't know because the team members haven't been selected yet." That's a perfectly acceptable response. If you are not ready to answer a question or complete an activity, set the workbook aside and do what you need to do so that you can respond to the question or take action. Or simply move on to the next question or activity and come back when you are ready. What's important is that you come back to everything that you skipped.

Becoming a better leader requires doing something for each of The Five Practices. You may be better at some than others, but you still have to develop your capacity to execute in all of them. It's like participating in a pentathlon. Once you begin, you can't opt out of any of the five events. You may feel that you are better prepared for some of the events than for others, but you must still participate in all five.

CHAPTER 2

The Five Practices of Exemplary Leadership

WE'VE BEEN CONDUCTING INTENSIVE RESEARCH on leadership since 1982. During that entire time, we have consistently chosen not to focus on the people in positions of power who make headlines. Instead, we've always wanted to know what the vast majority of leaders do—those ordinary people who make extraordinary things happen in organizations. To that end, we have concentrated our research on the everyday people who lead project teams, manage departments, administer schools, organize community groups, and volunteer for student and civic organizations.

To conduct our research, we've asked thousands of people, in writing and in interviews, to tell us about their Personal-Best Leadership Experiences. We asked each person to select a project, program, or significant event that they believed represented their own "best practices" leadership experience—the one they personally recalled when thinking about a peak leadership performance.

Despite the differences in people's individual stories, their Personal-Best Leadership Experiences revealed similar patterns of action. We found that when leaders are at their personal best, they engage in The Five Practices of Exemplary Leadership®. They:

- Model the Way

- Inspire a Shared Vision

- Challenge the Process

- Enable Others to Act

- Encourage the Heart

Let's take a brief look at each of these practices before you apply them to a project of your own.

MODEL THE WAY

Titles are granted, but it's your behavior that wins you respect. If you want to gain commitment and achieve the highest standards, you must be a model of the behavior that you expect of others.

To model effectively, you must first be clear about your guiding principles. As a leader, you are supposed to stand up for your beliefs, so you had better have some solid beliefs to stand up for. The first commitments you must make, then, are to *clarify values by finding your voice* and to *affirm shared values* and express them in a style that is authentically your own.

Eloquent speeches about your personal values are not nearly enough. Your deeds are far more important than your words when expressing how serious you are about what you say, and your words and deeds must be consistent. Exemplary *leaders set the example by aligning actions with shared values.* You go first by setting the example through daily actions that demonstrate you are deeply committed to your beliefs. You take the actions necessary to build consensus around shared values. You can't impose your values on others, no matter how hard you try or how much power you have. Unless values are shared among all those who work together, intense commitment is impossible. What you get instead is simply compliance.

The personal-best projects we heard about were all distinguished by relentless effort, steadfastness, competence, and attention to detail. We were struck by how the actions leaders took to set the example were often simple things. Sure, leaders had operational and strategic plans, but the actions they described were all the day-to-day things they did to practice what they preached.

You set the example by spending time with someone, working side by side with colleagues, telling stories that make the values come alive, being highly visible during times of uncertainty, and asking questions to help people to think about values and priorities. *Model the Way* is essentially about earning the right and the respect to lead through direct individual involvement and action. People have to believe in the messenger or they won't pay attention to the message. They first follow the person, then the plan.

INSPIRE A SHARED VISION

In describing their Personal-Best Leadership Experiences, people recounted times when they imagined an exciting, highly attractive future for their organization. They had visions and dreams of what could be. They had absolute and total personal belief in those dreams, and they were confident in their abilities to make extraordinary things happen. Every organization, every social movement, begins with a vision: it is the force that energizes the creation of the future.

Leaders *envision the future by imagining exciting and ennobling possibilities*. They gaze across the horizon of time, imagining the attractive opportunities that are in store once they and their constituents arrive at the final destination. Leaders have a desire to make something happen, to change how things are, to create something that no one else has ever created before.

Before they even begin a project, leaders need both a realistic sense of the past and a clear vision of what success should look like. They draw on the lessons from what has gone before, and they communicate a clear view of the future that pulls them forward.

Yet a vision seen only by a leader is insufficient to create an organized movement or significant change. People want to be involved in this process.

You can't command commitment; you have to inspire it. You have to *enlist others in a common vision by appealing to shared aspirations*.

To enlist people in a vision, you must know your constituents and be able to relate to them in ways that energize and uplift them. People must believe that their leaders understand their needs and have their interests at heart. Only through an intimate knowledge of their dreams, hopes, aspirations, visions, and values are you able to enlist support. Leadership is a dialogue, not a monologue. In these times of rapid change and uncertainty, people want to follow those who can see beyond today's difficulties and imagine a brighter future. Leaders breathe life into the hopes and dreams of others and enable them to see the exciting possibilities that tomorrow holds. To embrace the vision and make it their own, people have to see themselves as part of that vision and as able to contribute to its realization. Clearly expressing your enthusiasm and excitement for the shared vision ignites the same passion in others.

Without exception, the leaders we have studied reported that they were incredibly enthusiastic about their personal-best projects. Their own excitement was catching; it spread from leader to constituents. Their belief in and commitment to the vision were the sparks that ignited the flame of inspiration.

CHALLENGE THE PROCESS

Challenge is the crucible for greatness. The leaders we studied did not sit idle, waiting for fate to smile upon them; they ventured out. None achieved their personal best by keeping things the same. Instead, all their personal bests involved some kind of challenge, and all the leaders embraced the challenge as an opportunity to grow, innovate, and improve. Whatever the challenge—developing a new product or business, shaping a groundbreaking piece of legislation, or turning around a failing school—every personal-best experience involved a change from the status quo. Not one person claimed to have done their personal best by keeping things the same. All leaders break the "business-as-usual" mold.

Leaders are pioneers—people who are willing to step out into the unknown. They *search for opportunities* by *seizing the initiative and by looking outward for innovative ways to improve*.

But it's impossible for any leader to be the only creator or originator of new products, services, or processes. Product and service innovations tend to come from customers, clients, vendors, people in the labs, and people on the front lines, while process innovations tend to come from the people doing the work. Leaders know that innovation comes more from listening than from telling. They are constantly looking outside of themselves and their organization for new ideas and new ways of doing things, and they are willing to challenge the system in order to make extraordinary things happen.

Leaders also know that innovation and change require them to *experiment and take risks by constantly generating small wins and learning from experience*. Incremental steps and little victories one after another build enough confidence to meet even the biggest challenges and strengthen commitment to the long-term future. But not everyone is equally comfortable with risk and uncertainty. You also must pay attention to the capacity of your constituents to take control of challenging situations and become fully committed to change.

Yet even the most prepared and skilled people never succeed at 100 percent of what they do, especially when they are taking big risks and experimenting with new, untried concepts and methods. Risk and experimentation are always accompanied by mistakes and failure. The key that unlocks the door to opportunity is learning. Great leaders are great learners. They learn from their failures as well as their successes, and they create a climate in which they can help others do the same

ENABLE OTHERS TO ACT

Grand dreams do not become significant realities through the actions of a single leader. Leadership is a team effort. After reviewing thousands of Personal-Best Leadership Experiences, we developed a simple test to detect whether someone is on the road to becoming a leader: the frequency with which they use the word *we* rather than *I*.

Exemplary leaders Enable Others to Act. They *foster collaboration by building trust and facilitating relationships*. This sense of teamwork goes far beyond a few direct reports or close confidants. As the need for more inclusiveness grows, organizations become more global, and work-from-anywhere becomes more common, you need to find ways to connect with more diverse and often far-flung constituents. You have to engage everyone who must make the project work—and in some way, all those who must live with the results.

Leaders make it possible for others to do good work. They know that no one does their best when feeling weak, incompetent, or alienated. When you *strengthen others by increasing self-determination and developing competence*, they are more likely to be engaged and produce exceptional results. Exemplary leaders work to make people feel strong, capable, and committed. They don't hoard their power; they give it away.

In the personal-best cases we analyzed, leaders proudly discussed teamwork, trust, and empowerment as essential elements of their efforts. Focusing on serving others' needs helps to build trust in you as a leader. When people trust their leaders and one another, they are more able to take risks and use their energy to produce extraordinary results.

ENCOURAGE THE HEART

The climb to the top is arduous and steep. People become exhausted, frustrated, and disenchanted. They are often tempted to give up. Leaders Encourage the Heart of their constituents to carry on. Genuine acts of caring uplift the spirit and draw people forward. No one likes to be taken for granted.

Leaders *recognize contributions by showing appreciation for individual excellence*. In the personal-best cases we collected, there were thousands of examples of individual recognition and group celebration, from handwritten thank-you notes to marching bands to elaborate "This Is Your Life" ceremonies.

Being a leader not only requires showing appreciation for people's contributions, leaders also create a culture of *celebrating the values and victories by creating a spirit of community*. Celebrations are not all about fun and games, although there is a lot of fun and there are a lot of games when you Encourage the Hearts of your constituents. Neither are they about pretentious ceremonies designed to create a phony sense of camaraderie. When people observe a charlatan making noisy affectations, they turn away in disgust. Encouragement is curiously serious business. It's how leaders visibly and behaviorally link rewards with performance. When done authentically and from the heart, celebrations build a sense of collective identity and community spirit that can carry a group through extraordinarily tough times.

When striving to raise quality, recover from disaster, start up a new service, or make dramatic change of any kind, leaders make sure people see the benefit of the behavior that's aligned with cherished values, including reminders that success is a function of everyone's efforts and achieved through working together as a team.

THE FIVE PRACTICES AND TEN COMMITMENTS OF LEADERSHIP

Embedded in The Five Practices of Exemplary Leadership® are behaviors that can serve as the basis for learning to lead. We call these The Ten Commitments of Leadership. The Five Practices and The Ten Commitments serve as the structure for this workbook and the foundation for the activities. You will apply them to your project in the chapters that follow.

Take a look at the following page for a summary of The Five Practices and The Ten Commitments. They're what leaders use to make extraordinary things happen in organizations. Let them be your guide on your journey to success.

TABLE 2.1 THE FIVE PRACTICES AND TEN COMMITMENTS OF EXEMPLARY LEADERSHIP	
Model the Way 	1. Clarify values by finding your voice and affirming shared values. 2. Set the example by aligning actions with shared values.
Inspire a Shared Vision	3. Envision the future by imagining exciting and ennobling possibilities. 4. Enlist others in a common vision by appealing to shared aspirations.
Challenge the Process	5. Search for opportunities by seizing the initiative and by looking outward for innovative ways to improve. 6. Experiment and take risks by constantly generating small wins and learning from experience.
Enable Others to Act 	7. Foster collaboration by building trust and facilitating relationships. 8. Strengthen others by increasing self-determination and developing competence.
Encourage the Heart 	9. Recognize contributions by showing appreciation for individual excellence. 10. Celebrate the values and victories by creating a spirit of community.

CHAPTER 3

Selecting Your Personal-Best Leadership Project

IN TODAY'S ORGANIZATIONS projects are the most common way people organize their efforts. Publishing this workbook is a project. Getting a new product launched is a project. Replacing an outdated security system is a project. Remodeling your house is a project. Putting on this year's management conference is a project. Raising funds for a new homeless shelter is a project. Some projects are small projects within big projects, and one project often leads to another. So we'd like you to begin *The Leadership Challenge Workbook* process by selecting a real-world leadership project as the framework for applying The Five Practices.

Your leadership project should meet these six basic criteria:

- *The project is about changing business as usual.* Although some projects are about keeping things the same, those are not leadership projects. Select a project that involves starting something new or making meaningful changes in how something is being done, or both.

- *You're the leader.* You may be a contributor on a number of projects, but for the purposes of this workbook, select one for which you are leading the effort. You might be the leader because you are the manager and it's part of your job or because you have been selected to lead by your manager. You might be the leader because you've been elected by the team or because you volunteered for the role. Whatever the case, select a project for which you are the leader.

- *The project has an identifiable starting and stopping place.* While there may be other things going on at the same time, and while other things may continue after the project is over, it needs a deadline.

- *The project has a specific objective.* When the project has been completed, a new product will have been successfully released, a new system successfully installed, the renovated restaurant opened, the top of the mountain successfully reached. Whatever the objective, there will be something at the conclusion of the project that everyone can point to and say, "We did it!"

- *The project involves other people.* There are projects you can do by yourself, but you cannot do a leadership project alone. It takes a team to make extraordinary things happen in organizations.

- *The project is about to start or has just started.* While you should seek to improve your leadership in whatever you do, for purposes of this activity you should select something that is not too far along in the process. You will find this workbook more useful if you pick a project that's just getting underway or will soon launch.

Here are some examples of projects that are candidates for the process in this workbook:

- You need to institute a new customer relationship management system and expect to face some resistance.

- You have been assigned to turn around a factory that's had a history of poor labor–management relations.

- You are the leader of a volunteer team tasked with creating and implementing a countywide environmental cleanup campaign.

- You are heading a team responsible for instituting a new teacher development program for grades K–8.

- You are the leader of a task force that will develop your organization's first diversity, equity, and inclusion policies and practices.

- You have volunteered to rebuild the website for a local program that helps new immigrants find housing, learn English, and prepare to enter the workforce.

In addition to the six criteria we've listed above, there's one other thing to keep in mind. This is a Personal-Best Leadership Project, and you're setting out to perform at your highest levels. Select a project that represents *a significant challenge for you*. We know from our research that challenge is the opportunity for greatness. Challenge gives you the opportunity to do your best, and you are much more likely to do your best when you're stretched to exceed what you've done before. Of course, only you can determine what a stretch is for you, but for the purposes of this process, avoid selecting a project that feels familiar, comfortable, and easy to complete.

Now use the Personal-Best Leadership Project worksheet that begins on the next page to describe your project. In the next five chapters, you will explore each of The Five Practices of Exemplary Leadership© in turn, with a focus on expanding and enhancing your own leadership practices as you complete this project. The questions and activities on these pages will be instrumental in your achieving a personal best.

MY PERSONAL-BEST LEADERSHIP PROJECT

Take a few minutes to reflect on your leadership role—formal or informal, appointed, selected, or self-initiated—and the various projects (impending or just initiated) you lead that meet the criteria outlined in this chapter. Your project does not have to be at your workplace. Remember what we said in the Introduction: leadership is everyone's business. As long as it meets the six criteria, your project can involve your community, religious organization, professional or volunteer association, or another group in your personal life. You will find that you can use this workbook for all kinds of change initiatives.

Describe the project you have selected to focus on while you complete the activities in this workbook.

_____

_____

_____

_____

_____

Now look at what you know so far about this project. (Remember, you may not be ready to answer all of these questions, so respond to those you can and come back to this section when you can complete the rest.)

As far as they've been determined, what are the *project goals*?

_____

_____

_____

_____

_____

What's the *time frame?*

_____

_____

What's the *budget?*

_____

_____

_____

What are the *challenges* that you face in leading this project? For example:

- Funding is limited due to an economic downturn.

- Based on your previous experience, the constituents are likely to resist change.

- Team members are very diverse, haven't worked together before, and don't know each other well—or at all. Half of them are also working remotely.

- The decision-makers in this organization have shown little interest in or support for this initiative.

Challenges for leading this project

_____

_____

_____

_____

_____

_____

Who's on the immediate *project team?* Include titles, positions, and roles, as well as what you know about each person that's relevant to the project's success. For example:

- Tiffany—Human resources representative. Resource for HR issues. Excellent people skills and intimate knowledge of who's who in organization.

- Haru—Senior software engineer. Responsible for supervising technical aspects of project; strong technical skills, very credible with engineers, highly creative and innovative thinker.

- Tyrone—Technical writer. Writes the documentation and manuals. New to organization, but very talented at making technical material readable for nontechnical audience.

Your project team
Team member:

_____

_____

Team member:

_____

_____

Team member:

_____

_____

Team member:

_____

_____

Team member:

_____

_____

Team member:

_____

_____

Team member:

_____

_____

Team member:

_____

_____

If you have more than eight team members, photocopy the previous page or continue on another sheet of paper.

What other possible team members should you consider? What other stakeholders have a vested interest in the success of the project? A stakeholder might be a peer whose support you need, your boss or another manager, a vendor, a key customer or client, members of your board, or anyone else who is likely to be directly impacted by what you develop or produce. What criteria will each stakeholder use to measure success?

Examples:

- Stakeholder or stakeholder group: HR manager
  Criteria for success: Morale is high and turnover is low.
- Stakeholder or stakeholder group: CFO
  Criteria for success: Project is within budget; financial reporting is on time.
- Stakeholder or stakeholder group: Clinical services director
  Criteria for success: State-of-the-art technology and processes are deployed; results published in a prestigious professional journal.

Stakeholder success criteria for your project

Stakeholder or stakeholder group:

_____

Criteria for success:

_____

_____

Stakeholder or stakeholder group:

_____

Criteria for success:

_____

_____

Stakeholder or stakeholder group:

_____

Criteria for success:

_____

_____

Stakeholder or stakeholder group:

_____

Criteria for success:

_____

_____

Stakeholder or stakeholder group:

_____

Criteria for success:

_____

_____

If you have more than five key stakeholders, photocopy this page or continue on another sheet of paper.

What are your current feelings regarding this project? List several words that describe those feelings, such as _excitement, dread, panic, anticipation,_ and so forth.

_____

_____

_____

What aspects of this project do you expect to be frustrating or difficult? List the specific aspects of this undertaking that are most challenging.

_____

_____

_____

Why is this project important. . .
To you?

_____

_____

_____

To your organization?

_____

_____

_____

_____

To others (for example, the community, your colleagues)?

_____

_____

_____

_____

_____

_____

_____

CHAPTER 4

Model the Way

THE FIRST STEP YOU MUST TAKE ALONG THE PATH to becoming an exemplary leader is to discover your personal values and beliefs. You must define a set of principles that guide your decisions and actions and find a way to express them in your own words, not in someone else's. You must find your voice.

Yet leaders don't speak only for themselves. They also speak for their team, organization, and other key constituents. Therefore, you must understand and appreciate the values of your team and find a way to affirm shared values that everyone will commit to upholding. Shared values give people reasons for caring about what they do, instead of simply following orders.

Finally, leaders stand up for their beliefs. They practice what they preach. They show others by their actions that they live by the values they profess. They also ensure that others adhere to the values and standards that have been agreed upon. It is consistency between words and actions that builds credibility.

To Model the Way, you *clarify values by finding your voice and affirming shared values* and *set the example by aligning personal actions with shared values.*

Here are some examples from the personal-best cases we've collected of how leaders Model the Way:

The manager of a manufacturing facility saw that housekeeping conditions around the site didn't meet the plant's vision of being a "World Class Plant." He painted the words "World Class Plant" on a two-gallon plastic bucket and began walking around every day picking up trash. Word spread quickly and it didn't take long for more buckets to appear. The process he started by his visible example soon became the norm and generated lots of new ideas about how to make the job of cleaning the plant easier.

A senior manager in a nonprofit that provided resources to seniors began her new job assignment by taking her management team on a "virtual retreat," a series of Zoom meetings held over a period of two weeks. The purpose was to develop a set of principles that would serve as a guide for all team members. The manager began by sharing her personal values with the team. Then she engaged the team in discussions of their own personal values. At the final meeting, the team developed a set of common values and made a commitment to discuss those values with all of their direct reports.

The president of a chain of neighborhood convenience stores does not just talk about the importance of employee satisfaction and work–family balance. On important national holidays, he and other corporate office staff members work in the stores so that employees can spend time with their families.

The division vice president of an electric and gas utility works diligently to demonstrate the importance of customers. She makes a point every day of talking about customers whenever she interacts with members of her team. The first agenda item in her staff meetings is always customer satisfaction.

The new superintendent of a large school district shared a document with the more than 250 staff members entitled "My Leadership Principles & Core Values." He explained that "investing time to pinpoint my leadership principles has been hugely beneficial because it forces me to abide by these standards in my day-to-day operations." He framed the document and placed it on his office wall where he can see it every day, and he looks for opportunities to discuss his leadership principles with staff, parents, and others in a variety of settings. He has found that most people appreciate his transparency and that many share his core values.

OBJECTIVES

As a result of completing the worksheets in this chapter you will be better able to:

- Clearly articulate your personal values to the members of your project team

- Engage your team members in a discussion of their values

- Build consensus on shared values

- Align your leadership actions with the shared values

Reflect & Apply

REFLECTION 1

Think back over the last several years and recall the projects you have been a part of, whether or not you were the leader. Identify the two or three that were the most meaningful, energizing, enriching, and fun for you. What would you say characterized these experiences? What made them meaningful, energizing, enriching, and fun? What made you want to continue to be part of them? Make a list of these attributes.

_____

_____

_____

_____

_____

_____

_____

What do the attributes you listed above say about what you value in the way projects are conducted? For example, you might say, "One of the things that I liked most about the project was the chance to work with some talented people on a project that was really cutting-edge. This tells me that 'teamwork and collaboration,' 'innovation,' and 'intelligence' are important values to me." Another way of asking this question is: "What values and what actions are important to you in creating a climate in which you feel both happy and successful?"

_____

_____

_____

_____

REFLECTION 2

Imagine that it's one year after your project was successfully concluded. You overhear several people talking about the legacy you've left as a result of how the project was handled. What two or three things do you hope to hear them say?

_____

_____

_____

What are you already doing to help create this legacy? What else can you do? If you haven't begun, what do you need to do to create it?

_____

_____

_____

_____

_____

APPLICATION 1

Clarify Your Values

The late Milton Rokeach, one of the leading scholars and researchers in the field of human values, referred to a value as an enduring belief about the way things should be done or about the ends we desire. Values are principles that are intrinsically important to us, and it's unlikely that we will easily change them.

Your values are the fundamental beliefs that guide your decisions and actions. It's absolutely essential that you are clear about and mindful of those values, because your personal credibility depends on it. So begin by clarifying the values that you believe should guide your actions during this project.

Identify Your Values

Which of your values are the most important for the success of this project? What principles do you want everyone on your team to understand and hold as priorities? Review the list on page 36 of some commonly held values, then add any values that you think are missing. Finally, put check marks next to the five values that you feel are most important to the success of your project.

- [ ] Achievement/Success
- [ ] Autonomy
- [ ] Beauty
- [ ] Challenge
- [ ] Communication
- [ ] Competence
- [ ] Competition
- [ ] Cooperation/Collaboration
- [ ] Courage
- [ ] Creativity
- [ ] Decisiveness
- [ ] Dependability
- [ ] Discipline
- [ ] Diversity
- [ ] Effectiveness
- [ ] Empathy
- [ ] Equity
- [ ] Family
- [ ] Flexibility
- [ ] Friendship
- [ ] Freedom
- [ ] Growth
- [ ] Happiness
- [ ] Harmony
- [ ] Health
- [ ] Honesty/Integrity
- [ ] Hope

- [ ] Humor
- [ ] Inclusion
- [ ] Independence
- [ ] Innovation
- [ ] Intelligence
- [ ] Love/Affection
- [ ] Loyalty
- [ ] Open-mindedness
- [ ] Patience
- [ ] Power
- [ ] Productivity
- [ ] Prosperity/Wealth
- [ ] Quality
- [ ] Respect
- [ ] Taking
- [ ] Security/Safety
- [ ] Service
- [ ] Simplicity
- [ ] Spirituality/Faith
- [ ] Strength
- [ ] Teamwork
- [ ] Trust
- [ ] Truth
- [ ] Variety
- [ ] Wisdom
- [ ] _____
- [ ] _____

Set Your Priorities

Because you hold many values, at times some of them will be in conflict with others. For example, let's say you identify a new technology that can increase your department's productivity, but it will also lead to some layoffs. In your decision process, you are likely to weigh such values as productivity and profitability against, say, loyalty, security, and respect for employees' family needs. This kind of conflict cannot be avoided. It's important to achieve a greater understanding of your priorities so you are better able to resolve those kinds of inevitable conflicts.

To help you be clearer about the priorities of your values, list the five values you selected as the most important on the lines below. Then distribute a total of 100 points among the five. Be sure to assign a numerical value to each of the priorities; if you decide not to assign a numerical value to a priority, it should not be on your list.

Value   *Points*

_____   _____

_____   _____

_____   _____

_____   _____

_____   _____

Total Points: 100

Now what does this activity tell you about what you feel is most important to you and the success of your project?

_____

_____

_____

_____

_____

_____

_____

_____

APPLICATION 2

Check the Fit

If your leadership project is inside a formal organization, there may be an expressed set of organizational values that everyone is expected to adhere to. We know from our research that it is not possible to be fully committed to the organization if your personal values conflict with the organization's values. So take a moment to do a fitness check.

- Does your organization have a published set of values? If so, read them. If not, there may be a set of values that's lived out anyway. For instance, you may observe that whenever something needs to be done, individuals typically go off into their personal spaces at home or in the office and work alone, implying that this organization values individual achievement instead of teamwork and collaboration. Another clue that working on one's own is an organizational value is that all awards and recognitions are given to individuals and not to groups.

- What are the values in your organization?

_____

_____

_____

_____

- If you're not clear about your organization's values, what can you do to gain that clarity?

_____

_____

_____

_____

_____

• Think about how your personal values relate to the organization's values. Where is there alignment? Are there any points of tension? Where do your values and the organization's appear to conflict?

Personal Value	*Organization's Value*	*Alignment? (Yes/No)*
_____	_____	_____
_____	_____	_____
_____	_____	_____
_____	_____	_____
_____	_____	_____
_____	_____	_____

If there appears to be alignment between your values and the organization's values, move on to Application 3. If not, determine how you are going to resolve the conflict.

One way to find a better fit between your personal values and those of the organization is to engage in a dialogue with your manager about the conflict. Another way is to talk the conflict over with your family or a close colleague. Sometimes you will find that the conflict actually results from a lack of clarity; sometimes, however, you can't figure out how to meet your needs and the organization's at the same time. Whatever the cause of the conflict, you must address it. You cannot model the organization's values if you are not fully on board with them.

☐ There is alignment. (Move on.)
☐ There are conflicts. I will do the following to resolve them:

_____

_____

_____

_____

_____

APPLICATION 3

Build and Affirm Shared Values

When you're an individual contributor working alone, you might be able to use your personal values as a guide. But when you are the leader, you need to consider your team members' values as well and make the transition from "what *I* believe" to "what *we* believe." Just as your values drive your commitment, their own values drive theirs, and we know from our research that commitment flows from a strong sense that personal values are clear and shared. That's why you must discuss values with your team at the beginning of a project so you can build agreement around a few core values that everyone can pledge to uphold. If you have not already done so, now is the time to talk to your team about values.

> ## NOTE
>
> If you have not yet assembled your team, come back and do this activity once you have.

Here's what we suggest that you do:

- Schedule a meeting for the members of your project team. (If the team is large, you might want to divide it into two or three working groups.) Explain that the purpose of the meeting is to talk about the principles that will guide your decisions and actions as you move forward.

- Before the meeting, ask every team member to complete Application 1: Clarify Your Values (pages 35–38)—the activity you used to clarify your own values. Ask them to select the values they think are the most important, and explain that you have already done this activity. Ask them to bring the completed worksheet to the meeting.

- Begin the meeting by communicating the values on your list, and tell the group about any conflicts and tensions that came up for you during the process of clarifying your values. By doing this, you are setting the example of what you expect of people, and you are also working to build your own personal credibility.

- Ask the team members to share the values on their lists. Hold any discussion until everyone has finished.

- Once everyone has shared their personal values, look for the values that the team members hold in common. What values appear on everyone's list? What values do a majority of the group hold? Where are there conflicts? For example, do a majority of the team members value teamwork and collaboration, but a few value individualism and independence more? Discuss how these kinds of tensions can be resolved.

- Close the meeting by working together to develop a brief "team credo" that articulates the values and principles that will guide team members' decisions and actions during the project. Ask people to print this credo and post it prominently in their workspace so that it remains visible as they work.

APPLICATION 4

Align Your Actions with Shared Values

"Actions speak louder than words" is a common cliché. Like many clichés, it is often true, and it is particularly true about leadership. The extent to which your actions are consistent with your words determines your personal credibility. And the extent to which your actions are consistent with shared values determines your *leadership* credibility. Keeping in mind the team's shared values, you need to make sure there's alignment between words and deeds.

As project leader, what can you do to demonstrate the importance of the team's shared values to the team members, to colleagues, and to management? Brainstorm two or three actions you can take to show your commitment to each value. Those actions might include how you spend your time, the way you deal with critical incidents, the stories you tell, or the way you ask questions and express yourself.

- *How you spend your time.* The amount of time you allocate to key values sends a message. For example, if creativity is one of the principles the team considers important to the project, you need to spend some of your own time in pursuit of creativity. For example, you might visit a product design firm to see how they stimulate creativity, or you might invite an actor to lead an improvisation workshop for the team.

  Where and how do you need to spend your time?

  _____

  _____

  _____

  _____

  _____

- *The way you deal with critical incidents.* Significant unforeseen events or episodes can be opportunities to demonstrate commitment to a value. Critical incidents are what we call "teachable moments." For example, being part of a team doesn't mean that everyone has the same working style. Even when they commit to the value of working collaboratively, some people will still feel more comfortable working on their own. The COVID lockdown, with its shift to remote work and virtual meetings, offered those people the chance to slip back into their preferred individualist working style. How—and whether—you stepped in to address this issue would have sent a strong message about whether teamwork and collaboration are for everyone, or for everyone except those individuals. What are some ways you can prepare yourself to handle critical incidents?

_____

_____

_____

_____

_____

_____

- ***The stories you tell about exemplary actions by others.*** We are all fond of stories, and telling stories about a member of the team who does something to live out one of the project values is a very useful way to demonstrate that you are paying attention to what's going on.

Who has done something recently to exemplify a shared value? Where and when can you tell the story about what this person did so that others can learn from it?

NOTE

If you haven't started or are just beginning your project, come back and answer this question later.

_____

_____

_____

_____

_____

- ***Choose your language carefully and ask questions that probe key values.***
  The language you use and the questions you ask are powerful ways to shape
  perceptions of what you value. Let's say your team values service to others,
  but the language you and others use is all about "What's in it for me?" After
  hearing that message over and over again, what do you think people will
  assume is important? Similarly, the questions you ask can stimulate action
  in a particular direction. If you want people to think about their commitment to the shared value of service to others, you could ask, "What did
  you do during the last week to help another person?"

  What key words do you want to make sure you use to signal commitment
  to your core values? What words do you want to make sure you avoid and dis-
  courage? What questions can you ask to stimulate people to align their thoughts
  and actions around the core values?

  Key Words to Use

  _____

  _____

  _____

  Key Words to Avoid

  _____

  _____

  _____

  Questions to Ask

  _____

  _____

  _____

APPLICATION 5

Select Actions

Review your responses to the questions above on your use of time, critical incidents, stories, and language. For each of your top three shared project values, select at least one action from the options you generated above that you can take yourself to demonstrate each of those values. If you cannot yet come up with an action for all the shared values, come back to this page later.

Value   *Actions I'll Take Myself*

_____   _____

_____   _____

_____   _____

_____   _____

_____   _____

_____   _____

IMPLICATIONS

What have you learned about yourself as a leader from the activities in this chapter?

_____

_____

_____

_____

_____

_____

_____

_____

_____

Based on your experience with these application exercises, what do you need to do in order to improve how you Model the Way during this project?

_____

_____

_____

_____

_____

CHAPTER 5

Inspire a Shared Vision

LEADERS LOOK FORWARD TO THE FUTURE. They hold in their minds visions and ideas of what can be. They have a sense of what is uniquely possible when everyone works together for a common purpose. Leaders know that bringing meaning to life in the present by focusing on making life better in the future is essential to making extraordinary things happen.

But visions seen only by leaders are not enough to make extraordinary things happen. They must help others to see the exciting future possibilities and communicate their hopes and dreams so that others clearly understand and share them as their own. They must show other people how their own values and interests will be served by a long-term vision of the future. By expressing their enthusiasm and excitement for the vision, through making strong appeals and using quiet persuasion, they enlist enthusiastic supporters.

To Inspire a Shared Vision, you *envision the future by imagining exciting and ennobling possibilities*, and you *enlist others in a common vision by appealing to shared aspirations*.

WHAT IS A VISION?

We define vision as an ideal and unique image of the future for the common good. A vision articulates a realistic, credible, attractive condition that is better in some important ways than what exists. To inspire others, you need to be able to state what's unique and distinctive about your vision. You need to be able to describe it so that people can picture it in their own minds—"Oh, I see what you're talking about!"—and talk about it in a way that is appealing to all who have a stake in it. Only shared visions have the power to sustain commitment over time.

Here are examples from our personal-best cases of actions that helped some leaders Inspire a Shared Vision:

> Every quarter, *an insurance executive* assigned each of her dozen team members three different publications to read. Some were meant for general audiences, and others were industry-related. She wanted the readings to be diverse, so her choices covered the gamut from popular music to science and technology. The task of each team member was to look for trends that had implications for their business and write one-page summaries of those implications for the future. Then the team members would meet to discuss their work and look for themes. This process of continually scanning the horizon for emerging trends helped the team stay ahead of the curve.

> A *vineyard manager* decided to bring his core team together and create a credo and vision statement they could turn to when things were uncertain. The values they developed became the foundation for a "guiding vision" for the organization. But it wasn't easy. At first, the manager felt as if he was giving up control of the business. He kept thinking, "What if their ideas are awful?" and "Will I get stuck with a direction I don't want to go?" But he ended up with people who were totally committed to the credo and vision statement because

they were involved in its creation. They felt empowered to act, knowing that they had a "constitution" of sorts to rely on in the face of change.

The volunteer coordinator for a beloved community bookstore learned how important it is for people to take pride in being unique. The bookstore was a cherished institution, but it was in disarray and volunteers felt little impetus to go the extra mile. A principal cause was the lack of vision and direction for the team. The coordinator coached the volunteers on ways to use the store's scarce resources more efficiently, improve financial practices, and provide better service to customers. To inspire them to bring the bookstore back to being the place where people loved to go, not just because of the great collection of books but also for the inviting vibe and sense of community, she reminded them of how important the bookstore was to people's lives. She emphasized how much the institution was relying on them to survive and how they were in an honorable position not just to serve as a bookstore but to be a community icon with an esteemed legacy.

The head of a community outreach program of a state university wanted to provide an educational and service opportunity for students to engage with issues and people who were unfamiliar to them. He traveled to San Francisco with a group of students for the school's first-ever "alternative" spring break. This group slept on the floor of a San Francisco church and worked at local homeless shelters. Each night they cooked dinner together in the church kitchen and discussed the day's events as they ate. After dinner they gathered to participate in team-building exercises, discuss social issues related to their service experiences, write in the group's online journal, and prepare for the next day's work. His fondest wish for the project was for students to return to campus with a new sense of passion and commitment to social justice.

A registered nurse in her new role as unit leader of a hospital intensive care/cardiac care unit was part of a team opening a new state-of-the-art facility. She brought the team's vision to life by creating a logo with a slogan and choosing a mascot, one that identified with their Canadian roots and symbolized the journey they were on: an Inukshuk, a stone landmark built by the Inuit Natives across the Canadian Arctic that denotes a spiritual resting place along a migration route to food or shelter. She also created a "passport" that included a map of the new facility and a checklist for working safely in the new environment. Those innovations, plus a mock patient setup room where the staff could practice using the new technology and equipment hands-on, brought the team's vision to life and lessened the anxiety about the move.

OBJECTIVES

As a result of completing the worksheets in this chapter you will be better able to:

- Articulate your personal vision of the future to the members of your project team

- Engage your team members in a dialogue about their hopes, dreams, and aspirations

- Enlist others in a common vision

- Communicate the common vision in an attractive, appealing way

Reflect & Apply

REFLECTION 1

Make a list of four or five experiences from your past that have been "turning points" for you—experiences that have truly influenced the direction you have taken in your life. These experiences can be from many years ago, or they can be from the present. The important thing is that they made a real difference in your life. Describe each experience in a few words.

_____

_____

_____

_____

_____

_____

_____

- Review the experiences on your list. Do you see a pattern? A theme or two that connects them? What's the pattern? What are the themes?

_____

_____

_____

- What do the patterns and themes tell you about what creates meaning for you? About your hopes and dreams for the future?

_____

_____

_____

_____

_____

REFLECTION 2

Imagine that five years from now you are attending a dinner honoring you as "Leader of the Year." One after the other, your colleagues, customers, friends, and family talk about the contributions you have made to the organization, the community, and to them personally. What do you hope that they will say about you?

_____

_____

_____

_____

- What you want others to say about your contributions is an expression of your own dreams. What does your description of what you want others to say tell you about the difference you'd like to make in the world?

_____

_____

_____

_____

_____

_____

APPLICATION 1

Find Your Theme

Focusing on the project you've chosen, what truly inspires and excites you about it?

_____

_____

_____

_____

_____

_____

_____

_____

_____

_____

_____

_____

- Beyond its business, financial, or organizational objectives, what higher meaning or purpose does (or could) this project serve?

_____

_____

_____

_____

• What future trend(s)—demographics, technology, and so forth—are likely to influence the direction of this project? For example, we know that workers from different age groups—Boomers, Gen X, Millennials, Gen Z—often differ in a number of ways in terms of their values and the way they prefer to work. These differences could influence your project in the sense that you will need to find ways to accommodate multiple sets of values and work styles and be prepared to resolve conflicts.

_____

_____

_____

_____

• What future trends are likely to influence what you aspire to achieve?

_____

_____

_____

_____

• What future disruptions—such as recession, climate change, war, disruptions in the supply chain, or another pandemic—could influence the success of this project?

_____

_____

_____

_____

APPLICATION 2

Check the Fit

As you did with your values, you need to do a fitness check with the vision you are beginning to articulate.

- Are you clear about your organization's vision? If not, where do you need clarity, and how are you going to find it?

_____

_____

_____

_____

_____

- Compare your personal aspirations for your project to the organization's vision. If there appears to be alignment between your vision and the organization's vision, move on to Application 3. If not, determine how you are going to resolve the conflict. For example, as you did with Model the Way, you can discuss the conflict with your manager or talk it over with your family or a close colleague. You might find that the conflict is a result of a lack of clarity, or you might discover that you are unable to figure out how to meet your needs and the organization's at the same time. Whatever the root cause of the conflict, you need to address it. You cannot lead others to a place you personally do not want to go.

☐ There is alignment between my vision and that of the organization. (Move on to Application 3.)

☐ There is a conflict. I will do the following to address it:

_____

_____

_____

APPLICATION 3

Discover Common Ground

Engage your project team in a conversation about the questions that you answered in Application 1. You can hold that conversation in a series of virtual or in-person team meetings or on a retreat. No matter how you hold the conversation, it's important to elicit and listen to each person's hopes, dreams, and aspirations. When you have finished these conversations, help the group find common themes among the individual aspirations by asking the following questions.

NOTE

If you have not assembled your team yet, do this activity when you have.

- What are the common themes that weave our dreams and hopes into one tapestry?

_____

_____

_____

_____

- How does this project contribute to the larger vision of the organization?

_____

_____

_____

_____

APPLICATION 4

Give Life to the Vision

The practice that most differentiates leaders from other credible people is their ability to Inspire a Shared Vision. You have to be comfortable talking about your unique and ideal image of the future. You need to write and rehearse your "vision statement," whether you will be delivering it to one person at a time or to one hundred.

You give life to a vision when you infuse it with powerful language, with metaphors, stories, word pictures, and other figures or statements. Think of a vision as a song. If a song were about the theme of "caring," it would be pretty hard to sell if it just repeated that one word over and over again. All songs that stand the test of time are variations on a theme, and the words in those songs have a unique way of expressing that theme. Your vision statement needs to do the same.

The following exercises are intended to help you develop a vision statement that will resonate with your audience—one that will be remembered and repeated.

Before you write your own, here's an example of an inspiring vision statement that the manager of employee learning and organization development for a community college district put together:

> More than any other institution of higher education, the community college is in the business of changing lives. We meet our students where they are and help them define and achieve their goals. As they fulfill their potentials, we help them shine!
>
> In days gone by, the lamplighter dutifully set about lighting the streetlamps as day faded to night. We in ELOD light the lamps of learning, chasing away the darkness of uncertainty and doubt for our customers.
>
> When asked why he is so committed to this repetitive, mundane task, the lamplighter replies, "I do it for the light I leave behind."
>
> As learning and development professionals, we too are lamplighters, creating conditions that nurture the spark of new ideas and perspectives. Through encouragement, thoughtful questioning,

and provision of safe spaces for experimentation, we ignite innovative thinking and self-discovery in our learners.

The light we leave behind illuminates the paths of those we touch, enabling them to spread their light throughout the college.

Envision the Future

Picture yourself, your team, and your organization when you have completed this project. It has been successful beyond your wildest dreams. Describe what you see and hear in rich detail by responding to the questions and instructions that follow.

- What are people doing?

_____

_____

_____

_____

_____

_____

_____

_____

_____

_____

_____

_____

- What are people saying?

_____

_____

_____

_____

_____

_____

_____

_____

_____

_____

_____

_____

- How are people feeling?

_____

_____

_____

_____

_____

_____

_____

_____

_____

_____

_____

- What positive things are happening as a result?

_____

_____

_____

_____

_____

_____

_____

_____

_____

_____

_____

_____

Use Metaphor

The most powerful visions use metaphor or visual analogy to change abstract notions into tangible and memorable images. Here's an example:

Metaphor	How It's Like This Project
Skyscraper	Ambitious, expensive
	Reaches upward to the sky
	Requires a team and lots of coordination
	Requires different kinds of material to make it strong and beautiful

Take a few minutes to identify a concrete object or activity that could serve as a metaphor for your project, one that might be inspiring if your team and other stakeholders hold it in mind. For example, you could say your project is like:

- The New York City Marathon

- The ascent of Mount Everest

- The FIFA World Cup

- An eagle's flight

- The Blue Angels

- A huge, ancient redwood tree

Try this for yourself. First, take three minutes to brainstorm and list below as many metaphors—figures of speech that suggest a likeness between your project and something else—as you can.

My project is like:

_____

_____

_____

_____

From your list, select the metaphor that works best for you and your project. Explain how your project is like your metaphorical expression.

Metaphor	*How My Project Is Like This Metaphor*
_____	_____
_____	_____
_____	_____
_____	_____
_____	_____
_____	_____

Enlist Others

Now think about all the people you want your vision to inspire. Who are they? What motivates them? Be sure to include everyone you can identify: team members, customers, management, vendors, community members, and others. (See the example below.) Then list the motivators for each of the groups and individuals you want to inspire with your vision.

Audience: *Management*
Motivators: *Profit, future growth, competitive advantage*
Audience: _____
Motivators: _____
Audience: _____
Motivators: _____
Audience: _____

Motivators: _____

Audience: _____

Motivators: _____

Now review what you have written with one objective in mind: to identify what these audiences have in common. What can you do to appeal to their overlapping interests? For example, let's say one of the motivators they share is the desire for challenging and meaningful work. How can you help all of them find more meaning and make a contribution? You might talk about exciting opportunities to make a difference in their current roles, form diverse teams to explore innovative ways to make work more challenging, take field trips to visit award-winning workplaces, invite an author of a relevant book to speak to the group, or go on a site visit to another organization that is engaged in a related project but in a different industry.

What They Have in Common	*How I Can Appeal to This Motivator*
_____	_____
_____	_____
_____	_____
_____	_____
_____	_____

APPLICATION 5

Vision Statement

As a culmination of all the thinking you've done in this chapter, you are now going to write a compelling vision statement for your project. Do you remember how we defined vision at the beginning of this chapter? If not, take a moment to review. Then answer the questions below to formulate the key components of your vision statement.

What ideal inspires you—gives you passion—for this project?

_____

_____

_____

_____

_____

_____

_____

• What ideal(s) would inspire the other constituents on this project?

_____

_____

_____

_____

_____

• What is *unique* about the dream you and your constituents have for this project?

_____

_____

_____

_____

_____

- What *future* do you envision for your constituents and for the greater organization or community?

_____

_____

_____

_____

_____

- How does this vision serve the *common good*: the good of all essential constituents?

_____

_____

_____

_____

_____

- What metaphors or *visual image(s)* can you provide that would appeal to others?

_____

_____

_____

_____

_____

Now pull all the pieces together and write your vision statement below in four to seven paragraphs.

MY VISION STATEMENT

APPLICATION 6

Try It Out

Going live with your vision statement is like taking a musical to an out-of-town trial to work out the rough spots before opening on Broadway. Similarly, you need to try out your vision statement by delivering it to colleagues, coaches, family, or friends, asking them to play the role of "loving critic" and give you honest feedback.

- Who are some trusted people you can approach to "try out" your vision?

_____

_____

_____

_____

_____

- When will you do these rehearsals?

_____

_____

_____

- Whom do you know who is very good at Inspire a Shared Vision? Can you ask that person to act as your coach? (A coach is someone who can help you build your skills, not just give you feedback.) When will you approach them?

_____

_____

_____

• Once you feel comfortable with your statement and your presentation, select a time and a place or occasion to "go live and try out your vision statement." What is that time and place?

_____

_____

_____

   After you have made your vision presentation, how will you know whether your audience is genuinely inspired? For example, when people are inspired they smile, applaud, show excitement, and talk about how meaningful and unique the vision is. People might say, "This is the most exciting project I have worked on in ten years," "I never knew that something that seemed so ordinary could become so truly extraordinary," "I feel as if I'm learning," or "Now I know that I'm contributing to something really important."

• Think about the signals that will tell you people are inspired. Record those signals here:

_____

_____

_____

_____

_____

_____

_____

_____

_____

_____

_____

_____

IMPLICATIONS

What have you learned about yourself as a leader from the activities in this chapter?

_____

_____

_____

_____

_____

_____

Based on your experience with these application exercises, what do you need to do in order to improve how you Inspire a Shared Vision during this project?

_____

_____

_____

_____

_____

_____

CHAPTER 6

Challenge the Process

PEOPLE DO THEIR BEST when there's the chance to transform the way things are. Leaders seek and accept challenging opportunities to test their abilities, and they motivate others as well as themselves to exceed their self-perceived limits. Understanding that change is the work of leaders. They don't sit back and wait for something to happen; instead, they are always inviting and creating new initiatives to make things better.

But most innovations do not come from leaders—they come from the people closest to the work. They also come from what we call "outsight." Exemplary leaders venture out to find good ideas wherever they can. They seek diverse ideas and points of view, ask questions, listen, take advice, and learn.

Exemplary leaders move forward in small steps with little victories. They break tasks down and set short-term goals. Knowing that trying new things involves taking risks, they create a safe climate in which people can experiment, make mistakes, and learn from their experiences.

To Challenge the Process, you *search for opportunities by seizing the initiative and by looking outward for innovative ways to improve*, and you *experiment and take risks by constantly generating small wins and learning from experience*.

Here are examples from personal-best cases we've collected of how several leaders Challenge the Process:

> At the height of the COVID-19 crisis, *a nursing supervisor* realized that the patients' near-total isolation meant that they and their families could not be together at a time when they needed one another the most. She asked her team to come up with options for offering visual and audio connections to their patients. The obvious options included the iPads typically used for patient education, laptops used for medical record charting, and even the nurses' personal cell phones. Knowing that this was bigger than just her unit, however, she formally convened a task force, with her colleague from IT as their partner. Committed to finding a solution, the task force quickly created a virtual visitation and communication policy for all patients that included livestreaming, centralized device distribution, patient and family communication expectations, and a communication champion for each clinical unit. The usually slow pace of change and innovation typical of this organization was nowhere in evidence.

> *A new plant manager* was brought in to improve the quality of his plant's production process. In order to communicate that "things are going to be different," he had the floors cleaned, walls painted, and employee washrooms renovated. This grabbed people's attention, demonstrated that quality is in the little details—it's hard to produce quality products in a dirty facility—and made it clear that the new manager was serious about making things better.

> To increase the flow of new menu ideas and improve customer service, *the executive chef of a well-established restaurant* treats her servers and cooks to three meals at any restaurant similar to theirs in terms of size, cuisine, and type of customer. She then meets with the staff so they can share what they learned and brainstorm ideas for new menu items and improving customer service.

> *The new director of science and technology at a university* needed to increase the number of research grants coming into the university. He wanted his

faculty to more freely exchange ideas and engage in conversation so that they could come up with innovative ideas. His first action was to put blackboards in the halls and common rooms in the building so that spontaneous scientific discussions could occur anywhere and at any time.

The newly appointed manager of instructional design for an e-commerce firm was faced with a dilemma. Her team members needed to meet at least once a week. But not only did they all work remotely, they lived in different states, and a few lived in other countries. That meant nearly everyone was in a different time zone, so no matter when she scheduled a meeting, the time would be inconvenient for someone. After spending a couple of fruitless hours juggling time charts, she sent an email to the team, explaining the problem, including a list of team members' time zones, and asking for suggestions. After some back and forth, the group finally agreed on a time of day that was acceptable to everyone.

The new president of a charitable organization wanted to change the culture from one where people were reluctant to take risks for fear of failure to one in which everyone admits and learns from mistakes. So at the end of every project, he conducted a "postmortem" during which everyone talked about what went well, what went poorly, what they learned, and what they could do better the next time. He went first, openly admitting his mistakes so that others would feel more comfortable doing the same.

OBJECTIVES

As a result of completing the worksheets in this chapter you will be better able to:

- Identify opportunities in your project that would benefit from innovative approaches

- Engage your team members in generating and selecting innovative solutions

- Implement methods for learning from the inevitable mistakes of challenging the status quo

- Identify incremental steps you can take to implement changes and to create a sense of forward momentum

Reflect & Apply

Answer the following reflection questions:

- What have you changed recently about the way you do things?

_____

_____

_____

_____

_____

_____

_____

- What "daring failure" have you experienced in your life? How did you handle it? What did you learn? Be as specific as you can.

_____

_____

_____

_____

_____

_____

_____

• What do you find fun and rewarding about taking risks and trying new things?

_____

_____

_____

_____

_____

_____

_____

• What do you find difficult about taking risks and trying new things?

_____

_____

_____

_____

_____

_____

_____

_____

APPLICATION 1

Check for Limiting Assumptions

In every sector, industry, organization, program, and group, it seems that even before you start a project, there are real or imagined limitations on what you can do. You're undoubtedly familiar with hearing, "We can't do that because. . ." whenever you propose something innovative and different. Of course, some of the reasons for not making a change are valid. But some are simply emotional reactions, because change can be uncomfortable and even frightening.

Following are examples of common statements about possible constraints on your project. Check the statements that express what you are likely to hear when you propose a change. Then use the space below the examples to add any other reasons you might hear.

Examples:

☐ We don't have enough staff/space/money/time/and so on for this project.

☐ We're working remotely, which makes it hard to communicate.

☐ We have too many other more important priorities/commitments.

☐ No one on the team has the technical expertise for this project.

☐ We're having a hard time replacing missing team members so we can get our current work done, let alone do something new.

Other reasons you might hear:

_____

_____

_____

_____

_____

_____

_____

_____

- Ask your team members to make the same list.

- Combine the lists and send a copy to every team member. At your next team meeting, review each statement and do the following:

  - Put a plus sign (+) next to those constraints that are valid because of a law of nature, a governmental law, an ethical value, or other valid reason for not doing something.

  - Put a minus sign (–) next to those constraints that are not valid or may be valid but can be challenged.

  - Put a check mark (✓) next to those apparent constraints that you want to challenge in the planning and execution of this project. You may not want to challenge all the ones that you marked with a minus sign (–), but check as many as you reasonably can. Stretch yourself and your team to search for opportunities and experiment, but don't stretch yourselves to the breaking point.

  - Ask team members to post the final list prominently in their work-spaces. You and your team will come back to it again as you think of ways to Challenge the Process and more "We can't do that because. . ." assumptions appear.

APPLICATION 2

Look Outside

The best leaders and the most successful organizations do not assume that they have all the ideas they need. They know that the source of creative and innovative ideas on how to do things differently is more likely to be outside their boundaries. They are net importers of ideas. For example, to exercise "outsight" you might:

- Arrange a field trip to a place that would stimulate your group's thinking about what's possible.

- Read publications from industries and sectors you know nothing about.

- Contact three customers or clients and ask what they would like to see your group do that you are not now doing.

- Go shopping at a competitor's store or on their website.

- Invite an internal or external client or customer to one of your project planning meetings and ask that person to share their ideas.

What are some ways you and your team can search outside of your project and your organization to discover unexpected ideas? List them here:

_____

_____

_____

_____

_____

_____

_____

APPLICATION 3

Innovate and Create

Gather your team together to complete this activity. Explain that behind every apparent limitation is an opportunity waiting to be discovered. Say that you are going to ask them to think outside the box—literally! By doing so, they can transform how they approach any obstacle.

Share this example of thinking (and writing) outside the box:

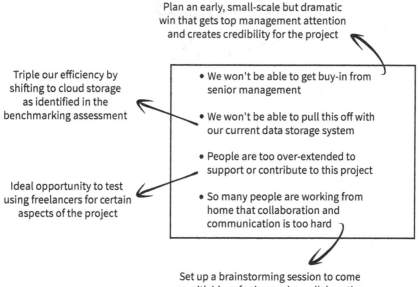

Plan an early, small-scale but dramatic win that gets top management attention and creates credibility for the project

Triple our efficiency by shifting to cloud storage as identified in the benchmarking assessment

Ideal opportunity to test using freelancers for certain aspects of the project

- We won't be able to get buy-in from senior management
- We won't be able to pull this off with our current data storage system
- People are too over-extended to support or contribute to this project
- So many people are working from home that collaboration and communication is too hard

Set up a brainstorming session to come up with ideas for improving collaboration and communication; before the meeting, ask each person to send you 3 ideas; pull those ideas together into a summary and review it at the beginning of the meeting

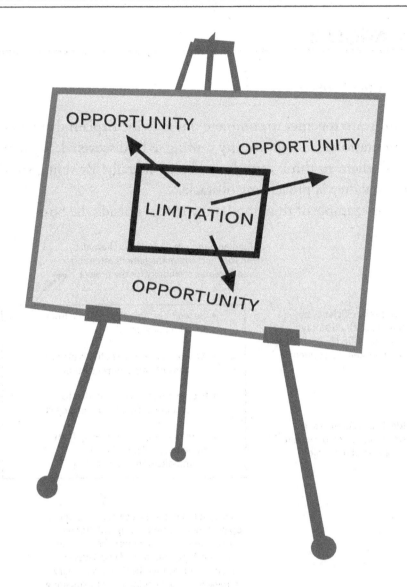

As a group, review the list of constraints that you identified earlier and want to challenge. Then follow the instructions below to Challenge the Process by brainstorming a way to turn each limitation into an opportunity to grow.

Instructions: Draw a box for all team members to see. Write the limitations you want to challenge in the box. Draw an arrow from each limitation to a point outside the box, as in the example seen on page 94, and come up with a way to turn each limitation into an opportunity.

APPLICATION 4

Check the Fit

Before you embark on making changes, make sure you and your team members talk about how what you plan to do fits with your shared vision and values. Record the ways in which the innovative things you want to do will contribute to the realization of your vision and can be guided by your shared values.

_____

_____

_____

_____

_____

_____

APPLICATION 5

Take the Initiative

As we said when discussing Model the Way, leaders go first. If you want others to be proactive in searching for opportunities and taking risks, you need to be the first to demonstrate those behaviors. Use the spaces below to write down what you will do during this project to take the initiative.

- The status quo I'll challenge and overturn:

_____

_____

_____

_____

_____

_____

_____

_____

- The experiments I'll try:

_____

_____

_____

_____

_____

_____

_____

_____

- The places where I'll look for new ideas:

_____

_____

_____

_____

_____

_____

_____

_____

- The ways in which I'll reward failure:

  (For example: You could give a Stuffed Giraffe Award when people stick their necks out, or an Edison Award for failing more than once on the way to inventing something new and different. You could give gift cards to people who "took a chance." Be creative, and send the message that you want people to take risks and learn from their experiences.)

_____

_____

_____

_____

_____

_____

_____

_____

- The immovable obstacles I'll demolish:

_____

_____

_____

_____

_____

_____

_____

_____

- Other things I'll do to take the initiative to change, grow, and make improvements:

_____

_____

_____

_____

_____

_____

_____

APPLICATION 6

Encourage Initiative in Others

Remember, you can't do it alone! You need to model Challenge the Process, and you need to create a climate in which others can do the same.

Ask your team members to answer the questions you answered in Application 5. They can do it as prework for a team meeting or they can do it in a meeting. What's important is that everyone participates in the process.

Before people share their ideas with each other, ask them to respond to the following question:

- "In order for me to feel safe in taking this risk, I need you (the leader of this team) to _____."

    Record the responses so everyone can see them and make a copy for yourself. Give team members one of the following responses to each request:

- "Yes, I will do that. No problem."

- "I can do that, *and* in order for me to do it, here's what I need."

- "No, I won't do that, because _____." For each thing you will not do, the team deserves to know a reason why. It's a sign of respect to explain your response.

IMPLICATIONS

What have you learned about yourself as a leader from the activities in this chapter?

_____

_____

_____

_____

_____

_____

_____

Based on your experience with these application exercises, what do you need to do in order to improve how you Challenge the Process during this project?

_____

_____

_____

_____

_____

_____

_____

CHAPTER 7

Enable Others to Act

LEADERS KNOW that they can't make extraordinary things happen all by themselves. Achieving greatness requires a team effort, so leaders invest in building trust and in developing enduring relationships. They know that as organizations become increasingly diverse and dispersed, physically and globally, collaborative skills are more important than ever to navigating conflicting interests and natural tensions.

Mutual respect is what sustains extraordinary group efforts. Leaders build the skills and abilities of their constituents to deliver on commitments. They create a climate where people feel in control of their own lives.

To Enable Others to Act, you *foster collaboration by building trust and facilitating relationships,* and you *strengthen others by increasing self-determination and developing competence.*

Here are examples from personal-best cases we've collected of how leaders Enable Others to Act:

> The first order of business for *a program manager in a multinational technology firm* was to learn how to trust her employees. She wanted to develop a cohesive and collaborative team, with trust as the framework. She began by creating an environment in which people felt comfortable asking questions and making mistakes. She talked with each person about mutual expectations and progress on key objectives, helped them develop working relationships with others outside of their department, and gave them ownership of and responsibility for their projects, along with the information, support, and training they would need. She then made sure to give them recognition for their work.

> *The principal of an underperforming school* needed to make some radical changes in the curriculum in order to improve student achievement. As part of this major project, he created an Instructional Leadership Team made up of respected teacher-leaders and gave them the discretion to determine curriculum. To show support for this team, at curriculum meetings only teachers sit at the discussion table. Administrators sit in chairs around the team to signal that they are there to support, and not to decide.

> *The chief information officer of a global technical, professional, and construction services company* was charged with rolling out a worldwide safety and leadership program to the IT organization—more than 800 people. Rather than leading the training sessions herself, or having someone in the training department do it, she asked everyone in the first two layers of the IT organization to lead at least one workshop. Everyone agreed that they got as much out of facilitating a workshop as any of the participants.

> When *the incoming commander of a U.S. Navy ship* took over, morale was terrible and performance was the worst in the service. He knew he had to do something immediately to turn the situation around. He decided to spend one hour with each of the 310 sailors just talking about themselves and their needs. In the process of listening and

paying attention, he not only built rapport and understanding, but he also gathered ideas about how to improve the ship that, when implemented, saved the Navy millions of dollars.

A manager inherited a very small staff when she took over an Australian program that helped local leaders set up, manage, fund, and lead successful social ventures. One of her staff members was very shy and had a real fear of speaking in public. He was happy to distribute the name badges at events, but that was it. He even feigned illness to get out of speaking engagements. The manager asked him, "How can we get you speaking in public?" Then she edged him toward it very gently. He gave a presentation to a small group, then to a slightly larger group, and then to another slightly larger group. In under a year, he stood on a platform presenting business awards to a large crowd. Afterward, he said, "Oh, my gosh, I can't believe I did it!"

An American financial services executive was appointed the managing director of one of its foreign offices. Because he was an outsider, he was viewed with skepticism. Rather than jump in with all kinds of changes, his first acts were to get to know people—who they were, what motivated them, what things they liked to do, and what they thought they could accomplish collectively. These early acts of relying on "local experts" quickly earned him respect and enabled all of them to significantly improve services.

OBJECTIVES

As a result of completing the worksheets in this chapter, you'll be better able to:

- Build supportive relationships with your project team members

- Develop the competence and confidence of team members

- Develop cooperative working relationships among team members

- Connect team members to the people they need to get extraordinary things done

Reflect & Apply

Think of a time when, as a direct result of something a leader said or did, you felt personally powerful and capable. Write down the actions the leader took that contributed to your feeling powerful, strong, capable, and effective—the master of your own experience. Be as specific as you can.

_____

_____

_____

_____

_____

Now think of a time when you felt powerless, weak, and insignificant as a result of something a leader said or did. What specifically did they do?

_____

_____

_____

_____

_____

Recall a time when you were part of a team that "just clicked"—a time when it seemed as if everyone was working together smoothly and effortlessly. Describe how people acted toward one another and what the team leader did that contributed to making the team work:

_____

_____

_____

_____

_____

_____

Using the lessons from your own experiences—as an individual and as a team member—ask yourself, "How can I enable others to feel powerful and avoid diminishing their personal effectiveness? How can I contribute to teamwork and trust?" Record your responses:

_____

_____

_____

_____

_____

_____

_____

_____

Ask yourself, "In what ways will making others feel powerful and creating a climate of teamwork and trust benefit this project?" Record your responses:

_____

_____

_____

_____

APPLICATION 1

Ask Questions, Listen, and Take Advice

Leadership is a relationship, and a healthy relationship is based on trust. Trust is essential for building collaboration and promoting the relationships that let people work together cooperatively. Trust is fostered by listening and attending to the other person. Demonstrate that you trust them before you ask them to trust you.

If you have not already done so, schedule a sixty-minute one-on-one relationship-building meeting with each of your project team members. During these meetings, ask a lot of questions, and listen carefully to their responses. Here are the kinds of questions you should ask during the one-on-one meetings. (Note: You might need to skip or delay some questions if the team has just been formed.)

- What do you want to get out of your experience as a member of this project team? What do you want to accomplish?

- What motivates you to do the best work you can?

- What strengths and skills do you bring to the team for this project? What can I do to help you sharpen your talents and strengthen your skills?

- How would you characterize the relationships among the team members right now? What can I do to help create and maintain a sense of belonging among team members? A climate of teamwork and trust?

- Do you think that we have enough diversity of backgrounds and perspectives on our team?

- Do you feel that our processes and programs are impartial and fair to everyone? What would you like to see changed?

- Have there been recent decisions that caused people to feel that they are not valued? If so, what can I do to make sure that doesn't happen again?

- What specific recommendations do you have about how we can do our best work on this project?

- What would have to happen during the project for you to be able to look back later and honestly say, "This was the best project I have ever been a part of"?

APPLICATION 2

Ensure Self-Leadership

After you have completed your interviews, complete a Power Profile for each person on your project team. Write down what each person needs, such as skills, resources, or support, so they can lead or be self-led. (You have our permission to reproduce the Power Profile on pages 114–116 for each team member.)

POWER PROFILE

Team Member:

_____

Project Role:

_____

What unique perspective does this person bring to our team?

_____

_____

_____

_____

Which of this person's strengths and skills will be most useful to our team?

_____

_____

_____

What kind of training and support might help this person become a stronger team member?

_____

_____

_____

_____

What opportunities can I provide for this person to assume greater responsibility or achieve greater visibility?

_____

_____

_____

_____

What information does this person require to work productively?

_____

_____

_____

_____

What opportunities can I provide for this person to work collaboratively with other team members?

_____

_____

_____

_____

What are areas in which this person could be more effective, and how can I help them improve?

_____

_____

_____

_____

APPLICATION 3

Develop Competence and Confidence

Review your team members' Power Profiles. For each person on the team, identify at least one action that you can take to increase their confidence and personal capacity to perform.

Examples

Team Member: *Janaid*

One action to enable this team member to act: *Feels powerful when he has the right information. Put him in touch with Jennifer in Information Technology for systems assistance.*

Team Member: *Sharon*

One action to enable this team member to act: *Feels powerful when she has strong skills. Says she has trouble managing her time. Send her to a course on time management and then provide the tools she needs to help her use those skills daily.*

Team Member: *Jose Luis*

One action to enable this team member to act: *Highly experienced in his field and feels powerful when he has the personal discretion to make decisions. Make sure to agree on what's expected at the beginning and then get out of his way and let him do the work. Set up regular sessions in which we discuss his progress.*

Team Member:

_____

One action to enable this team member to act:

_____

_____

_____

Team Member:

_____

One action to enable this team member to act:

_____

_____

_____

Team Member:

_____

One action to enable this team member to act:

_____

_____

_____

Team Member:

_____

One action to enable this team member to act:

_____

_____

_____

If you have more than four team members, photocopy this page or continue on another sheet of paper.

APPLICATION 4

Develop Cooperative Goals

Based on your interviews, there are likely to be things that all or most of your team members want from their experience during the project and want to accomplish through the project. What are the goals that people share in common? What motivations are shared?

_____

_____

_____

_____

_____

What actions can you take to build on these shared motivations and goals to create a sense that "We're all in this together"?

For example:

- Let's say one of the team's shared motivations is to learn from others. To help people do that, you can start your regular team meetings by asking everyone to report on something new they learned that week—a new method of doing the work, the name of a contact who is a great resource, or an effective way to reduce stress. Be the first to speak and share what you have learned.

- Let's say a common goal is to have the project recognized for its contribution to the field. You could ask for volunteers to document what is done and write a journal article and/or submit a proposal to present a paper at a professional conference.

- Let's say that a shared motivation is to reduce the time spent on the tedious routine tasks that are part of every project. As the project gets underway, you could ask the group to brainstorm a list of those tasks and elicit ideas for reducing or even eliminating them.

Actions you can take to build on shared goals and motivations:

_____

_____

_____

_____

_____

_____

_____

APPLICATION 5

Make Connections

It's not just what you know and what you can do that gets things done. It's also *whom* you know. For your team members to perform at their best, they need to be directly connected to the right people for important resources—information, materials, money, and so on. Your job is not to control access to those resources but to set up the connections and then let your team members deal with them directly.

One tool for helping you to map out who needs to be connected to whom is a *sociogram*. A sociogram is simply a graphic representation of the relationships in a group. There's an example in the graphic on page 122.

To create a sociogram for people on your project:

- Draw a circle in the middle of a blank sheet of paper or your collaboration tool. Put the name of a team member in the circle.

- Surrounding this name, draw circles representing the critical people to whom this person needs to be connected in order to do his or her best. There may be half a dozen or more critical people.

- Below each person's name, indicate the kind of "resource" needed. For instance, the resource could be information, money, the ability to teach a critical skill, approval, access to other people, and so forth.

- Draw lines to connect the people who should know each other or should be directly connected with each other in some way. If two people should be closely connected—that is, if they should interact frequently—draw a thick line to connect them. If two people should interact somewhat often, draw a thin line to connect them. If two people should know each other, but they have no need to interact directly, then draw a dotted line.

- Step back and see what this visual tells you about what needs to be done in this situation.

Look at the example. Let's imagine that Carlos is on your team, and he's writing a technical manual that is on the critical path of the project. Around Carlos are the individuals who are most critical to his success.

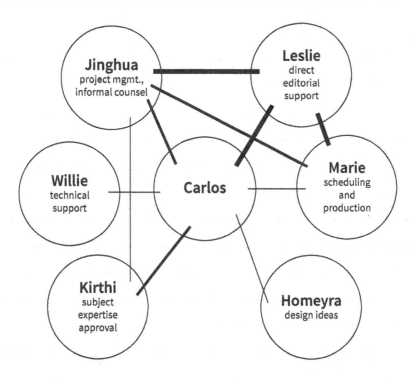

What does this sociogram tell you? It's clear that Leslie and Jinghua are the most critical people to Carlos in this project. Kirthi also plays an important role. If Carlos is going to do the best he can, he has to be empowered to work closely with these individuals. The sociogram also shows that there are critical connections that need to exist between Leslie and Jinghua; between Leslie, Jinghua, and Marie; and between Leslie and Marie. If you were the project leader in this situation, you would want to pay attention to these relationships even if you did not have direct control over them.

Now use a blank sheet of paper to draw a sociogram for yourself.

When you have finished your own sociogram, ask the members of your immediate team to create their individual sociograms. Then review their sociograms. What do you need to do to make sure that each team member has the critical connections they need so they can do their best?

_____

_____

_____

_____

_____

_____

_____

_____

_____

_____

_____

_____

_____

_____

_____

_____

_____

_____

_____

_____

IMPLICATIONS

What have you learned about yourself as a leader from the activities in this chapter?

_____

_____

_____

_____

_____

_____

_____

_____

Based on your experience with these application exercises, what do you need to do in order to improve how you Enable Others to Act during this project?

_____

_____

_____

_____

_____

_____

_____

_____

_____

_____

_____

_____

CHAPTER 8

Encourage the Heart

MAKING EXTRAORDINARY THINGS HAPPEN IN ORGANIZA-TIONS is hard work. Leaders encourage their followers' hearts to go the distance. They recognize and reward people's efforts in pursuit of the common vision and values. With personalized recognitions—a thank-you note, a smile, and both private and public praise—they let their team members know how much their work means to the organization.

Leaders also express pride in the accomplishments of their teams. They make a point of telling others what the team has achieved. They make time to celebrate milestones visibly and publicly, reinforcing the fact that people accomplish more together than apart.

To Encourage the Heart, you *recognize contributions by showing appreciation for individual excellence,* and you *celebrate the values and victories by creating a spirit of community.*

Here are examples from the personal-best cases we've collected of how leaders Encourage the Heart:

The new coach of a high school basketball team took the same team of girls who'd had a losing season the prior year and applied a positive approach to creating a winning season the next year. Her method was simple. Instead of always pointing out the negatives, she would start with "Here's what you guys did right," and then "Here are two or three things you can improve on." She also made it a point to tell the girls often how much she believed they could win, and she made sure that the team members stayed positive with one another.

The regional manager of a retail store chain would show up in person to congratulate the staff of a store when it had a week with great results. At quarterly managers' meetings, he would deliver awards to those store managers who had gone above and beyond in their duties. Instead of basing these awards on sales quotas alone, he found ways to reward people for stepping outside the box. For example, there were awards for most improved, most supportive, and even most courageous. He would accompany the presentation of the awards with a speech about the achievements this individual had made in their time with the company.

A manager with a global educational publishing company could sense that her team was getting frustrated and discouraged, losing energy, and willing to settle for mediocracy. She invited everyone over to her home for pizza and asked them to bring along a family member or a friend. As they dove into the pizza, she went around the room and shared a story about the contributions of each person on the team in front of people who matter most to them. By the end of the evening, everyone was pumped up about their achievements and roaring to go to the finish line victorious.

The chief information officer and vice chair of a financial services company came up with a fun way to launch a massive information-technology conversion at more than forty bank branches. A traveling team recruited employees at each bank to play roles in a skit designed to teach everyone about the conversion. There were executives in miniskirts, grandmas with pompoms, and employees dancing in the aisles. By eliciting laughs and spreading goodwill, the team made a challenging assignment, and the hard work that followed, easier for them as well as for the people learning the new system.

The head of a nonprofit agency with staff scattered all over the country came up with a fun way to celebrate his team's fundraising accomplishments: a virtual party. He sent balloons and snack boxes with cheese, crackers, fruit, and pastry to everyone in time for the party, and he suggested that everyone wear a costume. During the party, he asked the team members to share highlights from their fundraising project, such as the funniest moment, their proudest moment, something another team did well, the biggest surprise, and the best lesson they learned.

During the holiday rush *at one retail store, the owner* wanted to create a sense of community that would engage the temporary staff hired for the season. He installed a "Bragging Board" at the employee entrance, and whenever he wanted to acknowledge an employee for an achievement, he wrote a quick thank-you note and posted it on the Bragging Board. Soon employees started attaching their own notes of thanks and celebration.

A sales manager made a point of celebrating team members publicly when they achieved their goals. But one of his sales staff seemed very uncomfortable being singled out. He knew that the person appreciated a quiet "thank you," but he wanted to do more, so he bought a beautiful thank-you card and handwrote a note that included details of what the person had done that contributed to the team's success.

OBJECTIVES

As a result of completing the worksheets in this chapter, you will be better able to:

- Recognize individuals for their contributions to the success of the project

- Tell stories that will recognize individuals and reinforce key values and standards

- Celebrate team accomplishments

- Build informal social support among team members

Reflect & Apply

Think back over the times when someone has personally recognized and rewarded you for outstanding performance—the times when someone showed genuine appreciation for what you accomplished.

Select one time that you would consider your most memorable recognition—a time when you felt the most appreciated by someone. Recall the story in as much vivid detail as you can.

- What made this time so memorable? Why did you select this particular experience?

_____

_____

_____

_____

_____

_____

_____

_____

_____

- Make a special note of what the other person did to recognize you. What actions did they take? Describe the setting, the other person's actions, and your feelings:

_____

_____

_____

_____

_____

_____

_____

_____

_____

_____

_____

_____

_____

_____

_____

_____

APPLICATION 1

Recognize Individual Contributions

Recognizing and rewarding individual contributions to your project is your opportunity not only to Encourage the Heart of your team members but also to reinforce your project values.

In the chapter on Model the Way, your team agreed on shared values. Recognition for individual contributions to the project should always be framed in the context of those values. Recognition should also be personalized for the individual. Personalizing recognition makes it genuine because it comes from knowing the person and sincerely caring about them.

- Refer back to the list of values you developed in Chapter 4, Model the Way. Note what each value looks like in terms of on-the-job behavior. The best way to generate more of the behavior you want is to watch for examples of people who are doing things right. Don't wait for a special occasion to say thank you; recognize them as soon as possible.

- When you recognize a team member, link the person's actions to the value they exemplified. This serves to reinforce the value. For people who are comfortable with being praised in front of others, public recognition also provides an illustration of what others can do to contribute. For example, you might say something like, "The other day, I saw our project veteran, Kalisha, coaching new team members on how to use our new customer tracking system. She took time away from her own work to help someone else. I'll never forget what she said: 'I know you can do it! You're very talented.' Wow! Kalisha demonstrated to the rest of us our value of teamwork. Kalisha, come on up here. I know you love hockey, so the special 'Stanley Cup' [a tiny replica of the trophy] goes to you, along with these two tickets to the next home game of our local hockey team. Thanks, Kalisha."

- Check in with yourself: For you to help others do their best, you need to believe in their capacity to perform. Do you honestly believe that every member of your team is capable of acting, and will act, to achieve the goals you have set and live by the values you have agreed on? If you do, make sure you express it in words and deeds. If you do not, you'll find that you are going to have a tough time being very authentic and genuine in recognizing contributions. If you find yourself doubting the abilities of anyone on your team, take action. Talk with that person to learn as much as you can about their skills and abilities, interests, and particular strengths; where the person thinks they need new skills; and whether they think this project is a good fit. Find a strength on which you can focus and find the best fit for the person in the project. If people need to improve their skills, provide help such as sending them to a class.

• Getting to know your team members on a personal level helps you show appreciation in ways that they would consider "special." For example, some people love to be recognized in front of everyone, while others might find public recognition uncomfortable. If you do not already know what kind of recognition your team members would consider special, perhaps you need to spend more time getting to know them. Visit their workspaces. Check out the pictures and the curios they keep around them. If they work remotely, find the time to chat with the person one-on-one. Listen to things they talk about doing for relaxation and fun. It's all about spending time with and paying attention to the person.

As your project progresses, use the Kudos for a Colleague worksheet on the next page to think through how to recognize individuals who make a special contribution to the project by exemplifying one of the project values. Use this as a template each time you prepare for a recognition.

Completing this worksheet regularly is important. Research indicates that people tend to be more engaged in their work when they are recognized at least once each week, so if you have ten people on your team, you should do ten Kudos for a Colleague each week. That may seem like a lot, but once you get the hang of it, it should take only about three minutes per person. Don't you think it's worth it to spend thirty minutes a week getting higher levels of performance?

A note of caution: The purpose of these worksheets is to help you pay attention and note what people do that deserves recognition. It is not about filling in the blanks. The point is to be able to recognize others for their contributions to the success of the project. Use the worksheets as an aid toward that end.

KUDOS FOR A COLLEAGUE

Team Member:

_____

_____

The shared value that was exemplified:

_____

_____

_____

What did the team member do to exemplify the value? Be as specific as you can.

_____

_____

_____

_____

_____

How can I personalize the recognition? What can I do to make the recognition special for this person? Be specific.

_____

_____

_____

_____

_____

Where and when will I recognize the person?

_____

_____

_____

_____

Who else should know about this person's achievement and the actions they took to accomplish it? How can I let those people know?

_____

_____

_____

_____

APPLICATION 2

Tell the Story

We all have the potential to make a positive, lasting impression on others through the recognition we give and the appreciation we show. Look back at your own most memorable recognition—the one you noted at the beginning of this chapter. Someone made a lasting and positive impression on you. You, too, can leave such a lasting, positive impression on another person that years from now they will tell others that their most memorable recognition came from you. These positive impressions end up as the stories we tell others, not only as tales of celebration, but as models for future behavior that illustrate what's important to us and to others.

Developing your capacity to Encourage the Heart through the medium of the story lets you recognize not only that one individual. By telling stories, you dramatically and memorably illustrate how people should act and make decisions. Stories put a human face on success. They tell us that someone just like us can make it happen. They create organizational role models that everyone can relate to. They put behavior in a real context and make standards—the goals and the values that guide the team—come alive. They move us. They touch us. By telling a story in detail, leaders illustrate what everyone needs to do to live by the values and move toward the goals. They communicate the specific and proper actions that need to be taken to resolve tough choices. They bring people together "around the campfire" to learn and to have fun.

Write Your Story

Recall a time recently when you noticed one or more members of your project team contributing to the project's values and goals. Follow the steps below to write the story.

1. *Identify the Actors.* Name the person—or the people—you want to recognize:

_____

_____

_____

_____

_____

_____

2. *Set the Stage and Paint the Scene.* Where and when did this happen? Talk about the circumstances. What were the "actors" trying to achieve? What was their motivation? (To answer this question, you'll have to know something about them. This goes back to the need for leaders to pay attention.)

_____

_____

_____

_____

_____

_____

_____

_____

3. *Describe the Actions.* Relate in as much detail as you can what happened. What specifically did this person and/or each of the people involved do?

_____

_____

_____

_____

_____

_____

_____

_____

4. *Tell How It Ended*. Never leave your audience hanging. Tell the listeners what happened as a result of the person's or persons' actions.

_____

_____

_____

_____

_____

_____

_____

5. *Include a Surprise*. Every great story includes some kind of surprise. Try to add an element of amazement. What did you notice that was unexpected? What makes this story particularly interesting, unique, memorable, funny, or surprising?

_____

_____

_____

_____

_____

_____

_____

6. *Connect to Shared Values*. Every great story has a "moral" at the end—a values-based lesson about what people can learn from the example. What is the shared value (or values) exemplified by what was done?

_____

_____

_____

_____

_____

_____

_____

Tell Your Story

Now have fun telling the story. At a regular meeting or a special event, share this story with your team. A good story will only take three to five minutes to tell, and you can always find that much time at any gathering. What's important is that you authentically communicate how someone genuinely contributed to making the standards of the project come alive.

Once you've told your story, take a few minutes alone to reflect on these questions:

- What was the reaction? How did people respond emotionally?

_____

_____

_____

_____

_____

- How did you feel when telling this story? How comfortable were you? To what extent did you feel that your effort was forced?

_____

_____

_____

_____

_____

_____

- Based on the reactions of others, how well did you clearly connect the actions of the central character(s) to the values and standards you were trying to reinforce?

_____

_____

_____

_____

_____

- What did you learn about your ability to tell stories? What can you do to improve your storytelling abilities? For example, you could:

  - Attend the reading of a novel at your local library or bookstore. Pay particular attention to how the author constructs and tells the story. During question and answer, ask how the author got the idea for the story.

  - Keep a journal of things that happen on the project that will make great stories.

  - Listen to a recording of one of your favorite children's stories. Pay attention to how a professional tells a story. (We know that you're probably not working with children. This is about learning to tell stories, and children love stories.)

  - Take a class in storytelling.

  - At dinner with your family, don't just talk about your day, tell a story about it. Describe the rich details of place, people, and feelings. Let your home be your practice stage.

_____

_____

_____

_____

_____

_____

APPLICATION 3

Celebrate Team Accomplishments

Every project milestone is an opportunity for team members to celebrate what they have accomplished and gather the spirit and momentum to continue. Here's an example:

Project Milestone: *Marketing plan completed*
    Team Celebration:

- *End the day early, and have everyone on the team and their families adjourn to a local park where you can hang out, play volleyball, meet one another's family members, and relax.*

- *Invite a local comedian to put on a special show. Provide the performer with some "inside jokes" to include in the material.*

- *Celebrate at a virtual meeting. Ask each person to "bring" something they like to eat or drink, then play a game such as Clue or Trivial Pursuit together.*

- *Do a gift exchange—have each person send a $5 gift to another team member and open the gifts during the meeting.*

- *Invite a musician, a comic, or other performer to do a virtual performance for the group.*

For each of your project milestones, brainstorm several fun and meaningful ways for people to celebrate as a team.
    Project Milestone:

_____

_____

_____

Team Celebration:

_____

_____

_____

Project Milestone:

_____

_____

_____

Team Celebration:

_____

_____

_____

Project Milestone:

_____

_____

_____

Team Celebration:

_____

_____

_____

Project Milestone:

_____

_____

_____

Team Celebration:

_____

_____

_____

APPLICATION 4

Build Social Support

Public ceremonies serve another powerful purpose. They bring people closer together. In an increasingly virtual world where more and more people work remotely and much of our communication is via information technologies, it's becoming difficult for people to find opportunities to be together. But we're social animals, and we need each other. The COVID-19 pandemic underscored the importance of social connections. As we retreated to the safety of our own four walls, we invented all kinds of ways to stay connected with our fellow human beings.

Those who are fortunate enough to have lots of social support are healthier human beings. Social support is absolutely essential to our well-being and our productivity. Celebrating together is one way we can get that essential support.

Think of some ways you can encourage informal social interaction. For example:

- For people who spend time in the workplace, set up informal meeting areas with comfortable chairs and beverages that encourage them to relax and talk to one another.

- Put up a "Bragging Board" in a central spot in the office or on your online collaboration tool. Post a couple of thank-you notes, and then encourage others to do the same when they want to make a public recognition.

- At the start of every scheduled virtual, in-person, or hybrid meeting, begin by asking people to share something about themselves—their favorite color, favorite sport, a book they read and would recommend, a movie or TV show they like, the names of their pets, and so on. Get the group used to revealing information about themselves.

What other ideas can you think of to promote informal interaction?

_____

_____

_____

_____

_____

IMPLICATIONS

What have you learned about yourself as a leader from the activities in this chapter?

_____

_____

_____

_____

_____

_____

Based on your experience with these application exercises, what do you need to do in order to improve how you Encourage the Heart during this project?

_____

_____

_____

_____

_____

_____

CHAPTER 9

Reflecting on Your Personal-Best Leadership Project

THROUGHOUT *The Leadership Challenge Workbook,* you have been applying The Five Practices of Exemplary Leadership® to a real project in order to make it another one of your Personal-Best Leadership Experiences. Now that the project has been completed—or several significant milestones have been achieved—we encourage you to spend some time reflecting on your experience. Remember, the best leaders are the best learners. To grow as a leader, you need to learn from your experiences so that you can apply those lessons to your next project.

The questions in this chapter take you through the debriefing process for your own project. You can answer these questions on your own or you can gather your team together and answer them as a group. Or you can do both.

When you have finished debriefing, ask yourself, "What do my answers reveal about my leadership practices and about how I can be more effective as a leader in the future?" Armed with this new awareness, you'll be ready to tackle your next Personal-Best Leadership Experience with a better understanding of and appreciation for what actions and behaviors make a difference.

This debriefing carries an even larger consequence: it's a critical step in the continuing process of your leadership development. Take the time now to answer the questions below, and reap the rewards for the rest of your leadership career.

MY PERSONAL-BEST LEADERSHIP PROJECT

Review what you wrote on the My Personal-Best Leadership Project worksheet in Chapter 3. Then answer these questions:

- How did you assess your progress during the project? What criteria did you use?

_____

_____

_____

- Who else besides you evaluated your success? How did they measure it?

_____

_____

_____

- How well did you and your team meet the project goals?

_____

_____

- How well did your project meet the expected time frame? The budget?

_____

_____

- Which aspects of your project proved to be the most frustrating or difficult? Why?

_____

_____

_____

_____

- What surprised you along the way? Why?

_____

_____

_____

_____

- Write down several adjectives that describe how you now feel about the project (e.g., proud, exhausted, fulfilled, excited).

_____

_____

_____

- How do your current feelings compare to how you felt at the beginning of the project? What's changed? What's the reason for any change?

_____

_____

_____

- Overall, what have you learned about leadership that is a new insight? What have you learned about yourself and your leadership competencies?

_____

_____

_____

_____

Model the Way

Review the worksheets you completed in Chapter 4, Model the Way, and answer these questions:

- Which shared values were most important to you in guiding you along the project journey?

_____

_____

_____

_____

- How easy or difficult was it to forge consensus on values? Why do you think this was the case?

_____

_____

_____

_____

- Of all the project team's shared values, which two or three were the most important? How did you model these values?

_____

_____

_____

_____

_____

- What leadership actions proved to be the most significant in creating alignment between the stated values and the values in action? Which actions were the most important in creating consistency between values and actions? To sustain the alignment and consistency between stated values and values in action, what other actions could you take—or repeat?

_____

_____

_____

_____

_____

- What did you learn about Model the Way that you can apply to your next project? What would you do differently the next time?

_____

_____

_____

_____

_____

Inspire a Shared Vision

Review what you wrote on your worksheets in Chapter 5, Inspire a Shared Vision, and answer these questions:

- What higher purpose has this project served?

_____

_____

_____

- How does the reality of what you have accomplished compare to what you envisioned? How does it differ? How do you account for the difference?

_____

_____

_____

_____

- What metaphor would you use now to describe this project?

_____

_____

- What did you learn about Inspire a Shared Vision that you can apply to your next project? What would you do differently the next time?

_____

_____

_____

_____

Challenge the Process

Review what you wrote in all of your worksheets in Chapter 6, Challenge the Process, and answer these questions:

- What innovative methods and techniques did you try in this project, and how did they work out?

_____

_____

_____

_____

- What experiments did you undertake? What did you learn from those experiments?

_____

_____

_____

_____

_____

- What have you learned about being more comfortable with and willing to think outside the box?

_____

_____

_____

_____

_____

- What did you do to help your team members learn from failure and mistakes?

_____

_____

_____

_____

_____

- In what ways did breaking down your project into small wins—incremental "one-hop-at-a-time" actions—help you achieve your goals?

_____

_____

_____

_____

_____

- What did you learn about Challenge the Process that you can apply to your next project? What would you do differently the next time?

_____

_____

_____

_____

Enable Others to Act

Review what you wrote on all the worksheets in Chapter 7, Enable Others to Act, and answer these questions:

- Which enabling actions were the most successful? Why?

_____

_____

_____

_____

- Were the people on your team able to obtain the information and resources they needed? What actions did you take to facilitate that process?

_____

_____

_____

_____

- Write down some specific examples of when you gave power away. What effect did this have on your constituents? On you?

_____

_____

_____

- What did you do to make your constituents feel powerful? Was this task easier or more difficult than you expected? Why?

_____

_____

_____

_____

- What did you learn about Enable Others to Act that you can apply to your next project? What would you do differently next time?

_____

_____

_____

_____

Encourage the Heart

Review what you wrote on all the worksheets in Chapter 8, Encourage the Heart, and answer these questions:

- What form or forms of recognition had the most positive influence? Why?

_____

_____

_____

- What effects did recognition and celebration have on your team?

_____

_____

_____

- What creative means did you use to recognize individuals?

_____

_____

_____

- What was your most successful team celebration? Why was it effective?

_____

_____

_____

_____

- What did you learn about Encourage the Heart that you can apply to your next project? What would you do differently the next time?

_____

_____

_____

_____

_____

TYING IT ALL TOGETHER

Finally, it's time for some broader reflections on what you learned while using *The Leadership Challenge Workbook* to complete your Personal-Best Leadership Project.

- Of all the leadership actions that you took, which three to five do you believe had the most impact on the success of the project?

_____

_____

_____

- What would you make certain that you continue to do on your next project?

- What are the five most important things you learned about yourself as a leader?

- What five things did you learn about the members of your team that helped or hindered the success of the project?

- Which practice was the easiest to implement? The most difficult? Why?

- What do you feel are your strengths as a leader?

_____

_____

_____

- Where do you need to improve your leadership skills?

_____

_____

_____

- In addition to asking others to complete this workbook for themselves, how can you pass on your leadership lessons, especially to those you might be coaching or who might be candidates for leadership roles in the near future?

_____

_____

_____

_____

The Challenge Continues

IN THIS WORKBOOK, and in all of our discussions of leadership, we often use the metaphor of a journey to communicate the active, adventurous spirit of leadership. We talk about leaders as pioneers and trailblazers who take people on expeditions to places they've never been. We talk about summits, and milestones, and signposts.

As with most journeys, the leader's journey does not end with a single project. The journey continues with the next project you take on, and the one after that. As the ancient Chinese proverb says, "There is always a higher mountain." You know there will be more challenges along the path of your development as a leader. There will be more opportunities for you to do your personal best.

We hope that you will refer back to the questions we've asked you in this workbook. We hope you will use them the next time you face a challenge or discover an amazing opportunity, and begin to explore the possibilities of what you and others can do together. We hope you will teach others to ask these questions. And we hope that you will apply this process not only in your job, but also in your community, in your place of worship, and even in your home.

Challenge is the crucible for greatness. Given the daunting challenges we face today, the potential for greatness is phenomenal. There are no shortages of leadership opportunities, and your leadership talents are needed more than ever. We wish you continuing joy and success on your next leadership challenge.

Acknowledgments

IN THE INTRODUCTION TO THIS WORKBOOK we quoted Don Bennett, the first amputee to climb Mount Rainier, responding to our question "How did you make it to the top?" Now we think of Don's response when we asked about the most important lesson he learned. His answer was "You can't do it alone."

Sometimes writing a book seems like climbing a mountain, and it really is true that without the team of people climbing alongside us or helping out at base camp, we'd never have made it. In fact, this project began as a result of questions from the readers of our books and from participants in The Leadership Challenge® Workshop. "How do we put this into practice?" they persistently ask. We owe the most gratitude to them for their constant supply of new ideas and for continually requesting materials they can use.

We've always thought of The Five Practices of Exemplary Leadership® as both a process for planning change and a set of skills for guiding change. To help people use The Five Practices as a guide to change, we initially wrote a ten-page list of probing questions that walked people step by step through a real-life initiative. That initial list of questions was then transformed into "The Next Personal-Best Planner" by our colleagues at The Tom Peters Company: Homi Eshaghi, Lynne Parode, Christy Tonge, and Cathy Weselby. When it came time to completely revise the original text and create *The Leadership Challenge Workbook* in 2003, we were blessed with the talents of Janis Fisher Chan. Janis has also worked with us to develop this latest revision.

An extremely supportive, encouraging, and skilled group of professionals at Wiley have worked with us on this new edition, as well as on previous editions. Jeanenne Ray, our acquisitions editor and associate publisher, has guided this manuscript, among many others of ours, from the editorial process through to production. We appreciate her confidence, expertise, and perseverance. Michelle Hacker, senior managing editor, insured that the book made it from Word files to printed pages. Our copy editor, Amy Handy, applied her acumen, making sure that the narratives flowed smoothly. A shout-out to Jozette Moses, editorial assistant, for the important part she played in keeping us connected and on schedule.

Finally, our thanks to every one of you who wants to continue to pursue your leadership dreams, advance your personal skills, and make extraordinary things happen. Never forget that you make a difference.

About the Authors

JIM KOUZES AND BARRY POSNER have been working together for over forty years, studying leaders, researching leadership, conducting leadership development seminars, and providing leadership, with and without titles, in various capacities. They are coauthors of the award-winning, best-selling book *The Leadership Challenge*. Since its first edition in 1987, *The Leadership Challenge* has sold nearly three million copies worldwide and is available in more than twenty-two languages. It has won numerous awards, including the Critics' Choice Award from the nation's book review editors and book-of-the-year awards from both the American Council of Healthcare Executives and *Fast Company*. *The Leadership Challenge* is listed in *The 100 Best Business Books of All Time*, as one of the Top 10 books on leadership.

Jim and Barry have co-authored more than a dozen other award-winning leadership books, including *Everyday People, Extraordinary Leadership; Leadership in Higher Education; Stop Selling & Start Leading; Learning Leadership: The Five Fundamentals for Becoming an Exemplary Leader; Turning Adversity into Opportunity; Finding the Courage to Lead; Great Leadership Creates Great Workplaces; Credibility: How Leaders Gain and Lose It, Why People Demand It; The Truth About Leadership: The No-Fads, Heart-of-the Matter Facts You Need to Know; Encouraging the Heart: A Leader's Guide to Recognizing and Rewarding Others; A Leader's Legacy; Extraordinary Leadership in Australia and New Zealand; Making Extraordinary Things Happen in Asia;* and *The Student Leadership Challenge*.

Jim and Barry developed the widely used and highly acclaimed Leadership Practices Inventory (LPI), a 360-degree questionnaire assessing leadership behavior. The LPI has been completed by over five million people around the globe. Over 900 doctoral dissertations and academic research projects have been based on their The Five Practices of Exemplary Leadership® framework. More information about their publications and research is available at www. leadershipchallenge.com. You can also sign up on the website for their monthly newsletter.

Among the numerous honors and awards that Jim and Barry have received is the Association for Talent and Development's (ATD) highest award for their *Distinguished Contribution to Workplace Learning and Performance*. They have been named Management/Leadership Educators of the Year by the International Management Council; ranked by *Leadership Excellence* magazine in the top 20 on their list of the Top 100 Thought Leaders; named by *Coaching for Leadership* as two of the Top 50 Leadership Coaches in the nation; considered by *HR* magazine as one of the Most Influential International Thinkers; and listed among the Top 75 Management Experts in the World by *Inc.* magazine.

Jim and Barry are frequent keynote speakers, and each has conducted leadership development programs for hundreds of organizations, including Apple, Applied Materials, ARCO, AT&T, Australia Institute of Management, Australia Post, Bank of America, Bose, Charles Schwab, Cisco Systems, Clorox, Community Leadership Association, Conference Board of Canada, Consumers Energy, Deloitte Touche, Dow Chemical, Egon Zehnder International, Federal Express, Genentech, Google, Gymboree, HP, IBM, Jobs DR-Singapore, Johnson & Johnson, Kaiser Foundation Health Plans and Hospitals, Intel, Itaú Unibanco, L.L. Bean, Lawrence Livermore National Labs, Lucile Packard Children's Hospital, Merck, Motorola, NetApp, Northrop Grumman, Novartis, Oakwood Housing, Oracle, Petronas, Roche Bioscience, Siemens, 3M, Toyota, the U.S. Postal Service, United Way, USAA, Verizon, VISA, Westpac, and the Walt Disney Company. In addition, they have presented seminars and lectures at over 100 college and university campuses.

Jim Kouzes is a fellow at the Doerr Institute for New Leaders at Rice University and has been the Dean's Executive Fellow of Leadership, Leavey School of Business, at Santa Clara University. He lectures on leadership around the world to corporations, governments, and nonprofits. He is a highly regarded leadership scholar, an experienced executive, and the *Wall Street Journal* cited him as one of the twelve best executive educators in the United States. Jim has received the Thought Leadership Award from the Instructional Systems Association, the most prestigious award given by the trade association of training and development industry providers, and the Golden Gavel, the highest honor awarded by Toastmasters International.

Jim served as president, CEO, and chairman of the Tom Peters Company for eleven years, and led the Executive Development Center at Santa Clara University for seven years. He was the founder and executive director for eight years of the Joint Center for Human Services Development at San Jose State University and was on the staff of the School of Social Work, University of Texas. His career in training and development began in 1969 when he conducted seminars for Community Action Agency staff and volunteers in the war on poverty. Following graduation from Michigan State University (BA with honors in political science), he served as a Peace Corps volunteer (1967–1969). You can reach Jim directly at jim@kouzes.com.

Barry Posner holds the Michael J. Accolti, S.J., Chair at Santa Clara University and is Professor of Leadership with the Leavey School of Business, and chair of the Department of Management and Entrepreneurship. He previously served for six years as Associate Dean for Graduate Education, six years as Associate Dean for Executive Education and twelve years as dean of the school. He has been a distinguished visiting professor around the globe: Hong Kong University of Science and Technology, Sabanci University (Istanbul), University of Western Australia, and University of Auckland. At Santa Clara he has received the President's Distinguished Faculty Award, the School's Extraordinary Faculty Award, and several other outstanding teaching and academic honors. An internationally renowned scholar and educator, Barry is author or coauthor of more than 100 research and practitioner-focused articles. He currently serves on the editorial review boards for *Leadership and Organizational Development* and *The International Journal of Servant-Leadership*, and is a recipient of the *Journal of Management Inquiry's* Outstanding Scholar Award for Career Achievement.

Barry received his baccalaureate degree with honors in political science from the University of California, Santa Barbara; his master's degree in public administration from the Ohio State University; and his doctoral degree in organizational behavior and administrative theory from the University of Massachusetts, Amherst. Having consulted worldwide with many public and private sector organizations, he also works at a strategic level with a number of community-based and professional organizations. He has served previously on the board of the American Institute of Architects (AIA), Big Brothers/Big Sisters of Santa Clara County, Center for Excellence in Nonprofits, Junior Achievement of Silicon Valley and Monterey Bay, Public Allies, San Jose Repertory Theater, SVCreates, Sigma Phi Epsilon Fraternity, Uplift Family Services, and several startup companies. Barry can be reached directly at bposner@scu.edu.

Unlock the Power of Exemplary Leadership in Your Organization

We believe that everyone can lead with impact, no matter their role, when armed with The Five Practices of Exemplary Leadership. The Leadership Challenge® provides evidence-based leadership development solutions designed to help you grow, inspire, and develop effective leaders at every level.

 Inspire Leadership with Powerful Learning Experiences

 Gain Insight with The Leadership Practices Inventory® (LPI®)

Visit leadershipchallenge.com today to get started.

Index